The New History
of Political Theory

Garrett Ward Sheldon

The New History of Political Theory

Ancient Greece to the Modern World

PETER LANG
Lausanne • Berlin • Bruxelles • Chennai • New York • Oxford

Library of Congress Control Number: 2023933315

Bibliographic information published by the **Deutsche Nationalbibliothek**.
The German National Library lists this publication in the German National Bibliography;
detailed bibliographic data is available on the Internet at http://dnb.d-nb.de.

ISBN 978-1-63667-295-3 (paperback)
ISBN 978-1-63667-296-0 (ebook pdf)
ISBN 978-1-63667-297-7 (epub)
DOI 10.3726/b20744

© 2023 Peter Lang Group AG, Lausanne
Published by Peter Lang Publishing Inc., New York, USA
info@peterlang.com - www.peterlang.com

All rights reserved.
All parts of this publication are protected by copyright.
Any utilization outside the strict limits of the copyright law, without the permission of the
publisher, is forbidden and liable to prosecution.
This applies in particular to reproductions, translations, microfilming, and storage and
processing in electronic retrieval systems.

This publication has been peer reviewed.

FOR ELAINE

who has taught me more than any other philosopher
the importance of family love to human happiness and social justice.

Contents

Preface ... ix
Acknowledgments ... xi
Introduction: What Is Political Theory? ... 1

1. Socrates: Political Questioning ... 9
2. Plato's Perfect Republic ... 15
3. Aristotle: Classical Democracy ... 23
4. Cicero: Roman Law and Empire ... 39
5. St. Augustine: Christian Political Theology ... 41
6. St. Thomas Aquinas: Catholic Political Theory ... 49
7. Machiavelli: Power Politics ... 61
8. Thomas Hobbes: British Liberalism ... 69
9. John Locke: Natural Rights ... 79
10. Jean Jacques Rousseau: French Liberalism ... 91
11. Edmund Burke: Conservatism ... 105
12. John Stuart Mill: Intellectual Liberty ... 115
13. Karl Marx: Communism ... 125
14. V.I. Lenin: Imperialism ... 141
15. Sigmund Freud: Psychology and Society ... 147
16. Giovanni Gentile: Fascism ... 155

17.	Mihailo Markovic: Neo-Marxism	165
18.	Hannah Arendt: The Human Condition	175
19.	Robert Nozick: Libertarian	182
20.	John Rawls: American Liberalism	191

Epilogue: A (Possible) Future Political Theory: The Web of Globalism   201

Preface

At times of political turmoil and social change (such as our own), there is often an increased interest in various ideologies and political philosophies that underlie our systems and institutions. During the Renaissance, a renewed interest in Classical Greek and Roman thought occurred. In Modern British and North American political writings, a revival of the "Ancient Constitution" was visible.

Now, we see a rise in interest and investigation of historical Political Theory, to possibly clarify and illuminate our own times. A recent increase in attention to an earlier version of this book, originally published in 1988, seems to reflect this historical teaching.

The History of Political Theory: Ancient Greece to Modern America was a textbook for over 30 years in my year-long survey course on the Classics of Political Theory. It covered the major thinkers from Ancient Greece and Rome (Plato, Aristotle, Cicero, etc.), Medieval Augustinian and Thomist thought, to Moderns Machiavelli, Locke, Rousseau, Marx, and others, as well as the twentieth century "isms" (Communism, Fascism, Liberalism, Conservativism, Libertarianism, etc.).

These Major thinkers (or "Greats," as we say at Oxford) are known for discovering some aspect of human psychology, society, economics, or politics and having an impact on social movements, governments, and laws. While not always "good," they were influential: affecting millions of people, wars, revolutions, and civilizations. Familiar ideas of "justice," "freedom," "rights," "democracy," "equality," are given various definitions in these Great Thinkers, that inform even our present time.

The original version of this book was reviewed, read, and catalogued around the world and continues to inform intelligent political debate.

The college course in which it served as a textbook was part of the "Liberal Arts Core" and so was attended by many non (politics)-majors (in Science, Business, Arts, etc.) and it is gratifying that it was often received as interesting, informative, and accessible by people normally not interested in politics or philosophy. Nothing pleases a teacher more than hearing from past students that this study of the Classics helped them in understanding contemporary society and politics.

I am grateful to Peter Lang Publishing for printing it, my first book, 33 years ago, and to Lucy Melville, the Global Publishing and Editorial Head of UK/US for this new edition. Lang has always been known as a scholarly publisher of academic quality around the world and I am proud to be associated with it.

Gratitude is also due my Administrative Assistant, Sandra Jessee, and Student Assistant, Will Tanner, for help in manuscript preparation and permissions.

I am also ever grateful for my graduate education at Rutgers University, which had seven Political Theory professors on the Faculty (an extraordinary number) covering every historical period and ideology in Western Political Thought. It was a lively, free, tolerant debate of all subjects, leading to Truth. That Rutgers experience was the closest to true academic freedom and education I have ever known—expressing, hearing, debating all perspectives and learning the truth from that exchange. We looked at all sides with fearless detachment and objectivity, and trained our minds to reason, think, and understand. As Thomas Jefferson said of my later University of Virginia: "Here we are not afraid to follow the Truth wherever it may lead, nor to tolerate any error so long as Reason is left free to combat it."

And I am grateful to Oxford University (Trinity College, Hertford College, and Wycliffe Hall) for lecturing and research opportunities to develop and refine these ideas.

Our greatest hope is that more knowledge of these subjects will contribute to a better, more peaceful, and thoughtful world.

Garrett Ward Sheldon
Powell Valley, Wise County, Virginia

Acknowledgements

The author gratefully acknowledges permission to reprint from the following works quoted in this book:

> Plato, *The Apology* in *The Last Days of Socrates* translated by Hugh Tredennick (Penguin Classics, 1954, 1959), copyright © Hugh Tredennick, 1954, 1959.
>
> Plato, *The Republic* translated by Allan Bloom, 1968, Hachette, Basic Books.
>
> Aristotle, *The Politics* translated by T. A. Sinclair and revised by Trevor J. Saunders (Penguin Classics, 1962, 1981), copyright © the Estate of T. A. Sinclair, 1962, revisions copyright © Trevor J. Saunders, 1981.
>
> Aristotle, *Nicomachean Ethics* translated by Martin Ostwald, copyright © 1986 by Macmillan Publishing Company, copyright © 1962, Pearson; Celadon.
>
> Cicero, *The Republic* and *The Laws* translated by Clinton Walker Keyes, Harvard University Press and Loeb Classical Library, 1928.
>
> St. Augustine, *Political Writings of St. Augustine* edited by Henry Paolucci, copyright © Regnergy Gateway, Inc., 1962.
>
> St. Thomas Aquinas, *Political Ideas of St. Thomas Aquinas; Summa Theologica* translated by the Fathers of the English Dominican Province, copyright © Benziger Publishing Company, Celadon Books.

St. Thomas Aquinas, *Political Ideas of St. Thomas Aquinas; On Kingship* translated by Gerald B. Phelan, copyright © 1967 by the Pontifical Institute of Mediaeval Studies, Toronto, Celadon Books.

Niccolo Machiavelli, *The Prince* translated by Luigi Ricci, revised by E. R. P. Vincent, 1935, copyright © Oxford University Press.

Thomas Hobbes, *Leviathan* edited by C. B. Macpherson (Penguin Books, 1968).

John Locke, *Two Treatises of Government* edited by Peter Laslett, copyright © Cambridge University Press, 1967.

Jean Jacques Rousseau, *The Social Contract and Discourses* translated by G. D. H. Cole, copyright © George Weidenfeld and Nicolson Limited, J. M. Dent, Hachette.

John Stuart Mill, *Utilitarianism, On Liberty and Considerations on Representative Governments* edited by H. B. Acton, copyright © George Weidenfeld and Nicolson Limited, J. M. Dent, Orion Publishing.

Karl Marx, *Karl Marx: Selected Writings* edited by David McLellan, copyright © 1977, Oxford University Press.

V. I. Lenin, *Lenin: Selected Works I.*, Moscow: Progress Publishers, copyright © 1970.

Sigmund Freud, *A General Selection* edited by John Rickman, copyright © Doubleday.

Sigmund Freud, *Civilization and Its Discontents* translated and edited by James Strachey, copyright © 1961 by James Strachey, W. W. Norton and Company and The Institute of Psycho-Analysis and the Hogarth Press. *The Standard Edition of the Complete Psychological Works of Sigmund Freud* translated and edited by James Strachey.

Giovanni Gentile, *Genesis and Structure of Society* translated by H. S. Harris, copyright © 1966, University of Illinois Press.

Mihailo Markovic, *From Affluence to Praxis*, copyright © 1974, University of Michigan Press.

Hannah Arendt, *The Human Condition*, copyright © 1958, University of Chicago Press.

Robert Nozick, *Anarchy, State and Utopia*, copyright © 1974, Basic Books and Basil Blackwell, Ltd., Hachette Book Group, Inc.

John Rawls, *A Theory of Justice*, copyright © 1971, Harvard University Press.

INTRODUCTION

What Is Political Theory?

Political Theory and Political Science

Political Theory is a branch of Political Science. It is the original branch of Political Science and it remains the foundation of all other branches of Political Science. This is because Political Theory examines politics at its most general, abstract level. While other branches of Political Science, such as American Politics, Comparative Politics, International Politics or Political Economy study particular forms or relations of politics, Political Theory studies the basic concepts common to all political regimes and social systems.

Political Theory asks the basic questions that establish the foundations for all social and political systems. What is the nature of man? What is the nature of political society? And, what are good social relations? Every great political theorist explicitly or implicitly gives specific answers to these fundamental questions of human life and social existence. The history of political theory reveals a wide range of answers to these questions of Human Nature, Political Society and Social Ethics. Those answers establish the parameters of political discourse within each nation and explain the sources of antagonism between nations. The clarification of these assumptions of politics may contribute to wiser decisions within nations and more peaceful relations amongst nations.

Human Nature

How one defines Human Nature often determines the way one conceives of social, political and ethical matters. Human Nature is usually defined in terms of what distinguishes humanity from other species: what makes human beings unique and special? Is it our distinctive physiology? Scientists point to the human hand (with its opposable thumb and forefinger) and the human brain (with its large frontal lobe) as the most distinctive features of humanity. The coordination of hand and mind allows mankind to manipulate nature, to change the world in ways that other animals cannot. If you accept this physical and creative definition of man's unique nature (as both Locke and Marx, in varying degrees, do), you will conceive of society in terms of economics, production and engineering and politics in terms of the regulation of property.

An older definition of Human Nature focuses on moral knowledge. Mankind is distinct from other animals because of his capacity for moral choice and ethical action. Our Judeo-Christian religious tradition (Adam and Eve were expelled from the Garden of Eden for eating of the fruit of the knowledge of Good and Evil) and the Classical Greek philosophers adhere to this definition of Human Nature. That is why both emphasize a moral ideal, to which the individual and society should strive, and see politics as contributing to the realization of that ideal.

Other thinkers identify man's nature with an aesthetic expression: the ability to know and produce beauty. This conception almost combines the scientific and the moral conceptions, as it emphasizes creativity and identifies aesthetic sensibility with goodness. A state premised on this assumption would see art as an instrument of moral instruction and beauty as a standard of just harmony. The appearance of society, the appreciation and creation of a beautiful environment, would be the primary concern of a theorist defining man as an aesthetic being.

Finally, a key component of one's definition of Human Nature is how the individual relates to others. Is man naturally social or naturally solitary? Is the individual in society as an expression of essential human qualities or merely for private convenience? Should the state value the individual over the various groups (family, class, belief, community) in which that individual participates? Do associations have rights as do individuals? What is the motive for relating with others? The answers to these questions will often determine the way in which we conceive of and organize Political Society.

Political Science

Regardless of the particular quality that distinguishes the human species from other species, the political theorist must ask if society and politics are necessary to that quality. If a quality defines human nature and requires society to be fulfilled, we can say that society is natural to man and man is naturally social. This is the case with Aristotle, who defines man's unique characteristics as reasoned speech and moral choice-both of which require the cultivation and practice of political society. However, if man's distinguishing characteristic does not require society to exist or develop, man may be considered naturally solitary or independent. The thinkers who emphasize the individual, such as Hobbes and Locke, regard society and government as an artificial construct, a "social contract" made by free individuals to preserve their private benefits. Political society is not part of man's nature, but merely a convenience for enhancing his natural rights to "life, liberty and property."

The purpose and limits of the state will be defined by the origin of man's unique nature. If humans are purely physiological beings, requiring material resources and creating new inventions, the state may be limited to promoting and preserving the freedom, knowledge and property necessary to such pursuits. If he is inherently moral, the state may confine his freedom and his technology to conform to ethical considerations. If a society, like America, with multiple philosophical and religious roots, there will appear contradictory expectations and demands on society and the state, which will continually raise the issue of standards for right decisions, or social ethics.

Social Ethics

The moment an individual's will and social conventions collide or varying measures of right conduct converge, the question of ethics arises. In Political Theory, ethics can be broadly defined within two schools: Negative and Positive. Negative ethics emphasize what we should not do, if we are to be good. For example, "Thou Shalt Not Steal" is a Negative ethical statement-it says you are a moral person by virtue of not doing something. Negative political ethics tend to tell you to not violate others' rights to live, do as they please, and possess property, and otherwise to leave them alone. The good person, then, is someone who does not injure, kidnap, or steal from you and otherwise does not bother you. Positive ethics emphasizes what you should do for others. "Love Thy Neighbor as Thyself" is a positive ethical statement. It says that it is not enough to not injure others, you must positively help them to be considered a good person. The content of that "help" may range from giving them food to educating their innate abilities to restraining them from vice-which may violate their freedom and your own negative ethics. Both Negative and Positive ethics contain internal complexities, but in societies that, unlike the United States, draw from both standards, conflicts over standards of right are inevitable. Debates over a woman's right to abort a fetus or sell a child nurtured in her womb, society's privilege to demand military service from young men or mandatory schooling or workfare all can be reduced to conflicts over varying standards of social ethics.

And these standards of social ethics will correspond to different conceptions of Human Nature and Political Society. For example, if, with Aristotle, you conceive of man as naturally social and political by virtue of his capacity for reasoned speech and moral choice, then the state will be active in cultivating those capacities and justifying itself in terms of positive ethics. If, on the other hand, after John Locke, you conceive of the individual as naturally "free, equal and independent" by virtue of his physical condition, you will see the state as sharply limited to protecting private rights to "life, liberty and estate," endorsing negative ethics. The "great" political theorists are great, in part, because they present consistent views of Human Nature, Political Society and Social Ethics. So, when reading any theorist, one should ask two questions: (1) what are the writer's conceptions of Human Nature, Politics and Ethics, and (2) do they fit together in a consistent, logical way? Frequently, the great political theorists do not make their definitions of these concepts clear or explicit, being wrapped up in some contemporary issue, and the study of Political Theory, as in this book, is trying to discover their conceptions of these important categories.

From a thinker's conception of Human Nature, Political Society and Social Ethics will follow his definitions of other concepts, such as Justice, Freedom, Equality, Democracy and Revolution. These concepts become the general language of political debate, being filled with different contents at different times, and resulting in specific policies. Wars are fought and societies revolutionized over such words, so it may be useful to know what they mean.

Justice

Does justice refer to the treatment of any individual by the political or economic order or does it reside in the ordering of individuals in a harmonious, complementary way? Modern liberal and socialist justice tends to focus on the individual rights and benefits afforded by a society. Injustice, therefore, is the unequal distribution of either opportunities or goods to any individual. Ancient and Medieval forms of justice emphasized the individual's place within a larger order of unequal persons, classes, qualities, functions, etc. Injustice resulted when an individual was not prepared for his "place," did not have the necessities to carry out his function or presumed to leave his place and aspire to another. Both notions of justice, the individual and the social, presume a basis for determining either the grounds for rights or the designation of places and the people occupying them. Both go back to our conceptions of Human Nature and Political Society and each asserts itself in the American society in which we live, whether we are desegregating public schools or determining promotions in public employment.

Freedom

Does freedom consist in freedom from restraint (legal, moral, conventional) to individual desire, or is it freedom to achieve some substantive good (economic security, self-realization, fulfillment)? Americans, knowing little of either, usually demand both. But, given human interdependence, the realization of negative freedom may not guarantee positive freedom and the guaranteeing of positive freedom may negate negative freedom. For example, socialism provides individuals with the freedom to economic security, but inhibits the freedom from state regulation of individual enterprise, movement, etc. Capitalism provides freedom from absolute state control of economic activity, but not the freedom to economic achievement and security. Or, to take another example, American society has gradually lifted most legal restrictions on the "morals" of the individual, i.e., it has done away with most laws restricting divorce, abortion, pornography, etc. The abolishing of these restrictions on individuals' conduct is usually rationalized on the grounds that only the individual can know what is best for himself or herself and that such legal restrictions may actually prevent the substantive goods they are meant to protect (e.g., happy marriages, sexual fulfillment, etc.). But absolute "freedom from" restrictions do not guarantee the "freedom to" a quality life. The legal prohibition on divorce may not produce universally happy marriages, but the lifting of that prohibition does not seem to have accomplished that goal either. Without some positive rule enhancing the quality of life, negative freedom may liberate people from all social bonds without giving them alternative standards for creating their own.

Equality

After Freedom, equality is the premier value of our age. But what does equality mean? In mathematics, equality signifies identity or sameness. 2=2. Are humans equal in that mathematical sense? We look different. We possess different talents and virtues. How are we equal? In traditional religious doctrine, we are equal as creatures of God; despite our social and economic inequalities we have the equal worth and dignity of being equal in the sight of God. A more modern definition of equality is equality of material existence: we are the same in having physical desires, even if for different commodities. Out of that basic material equality derives our equal rights, equal opportunity and equality before the law. If all individuals are basically equal, the state ought not to treat anyone differently from anyone else. Under the U. S. Constitutional clause of "equal protection," America has seen the attack on all forms of public discrimination against women, blacks, gays, the handicapped and religious minorities. But what of our differences? Does the state concern itself with individual uniqueness as fervently as it does commonness? Aristotle claimed that it is as unjust to treat the unequal equally as to treat the equal unequally. This concern reveals itself in the respect for and preservation of cultural differences, in "gifted" school programs and value placed on uniqueness. How humans are considered alike and how they are considered different affects both politics and ethics.

Democracy

Democracy is the preferred regime in the twentieth-century world. Nearly every nation on earth describes itself as "democratic." The Greek definition of the term meant "rule by the people." But how do the people rule? Does every individual participate in every public decision that may affect his life? That may have been possible among the few citizens of the small Greek polis, but it is difficult to imagine in large modern cities and nations. Is voting for representatives presented by parties and the media democratic? Can a small party rule in the name of "the People"? And, to what end are citizens democratic? To prevent tyranny? To cultivate citizens' minds and virtues? To make sure everyone gets an equal share? To create a rich and powerful society? To create a good community?

Democracy may be the preferred regime of the twentieth century, but it was not always so. Plato ranked democracy near the bottom of his list of good regimes. Aristotle was suspicious of "the many" and saw excellence as a rarity. By looking at different conceptions of democracy and various non-democratic theories, we will better understand American democracy.

Revolution

Revolution, or sudden political change, remains a central issue for Political Theory. Is radical change healthy and beneficial or destructive and evil? Does it depend on the regime changed or the manner of change? Is revolution inevitable or can a regime like America's Constitutional Republic institutionalize peaceful change through elections and Constitutional Amendment? Marxists believe that a workers' revolution is inevitable and that liberal democracy will be swept away with capitalism and replaced by socialist democracy. What are the differences in these forms of democracy? Is there a way to make regimes more enduring or change more humane?

Political Theory asks these perplexing questions not because it holds single, absolute answers to them, but because the History of Political Theory offers many partial answers. More significant, perhaps, is that the History of Political Theory can reveal the basis of our own social and political order and help us appreciate those of other nations. As such, Political Theory is an active, uncompleted discipline, which can inform contemporary political debates and contribute to a more tolerant, peaceful and just world.

· 1 ·

SOCRATES

Political Questioning

The history of Political Theory begins with Socrates because Political Theory begins with questioning. Socrates (470-400 B.C.) was a Greek philosopher whose motto, "the unexamined life is not worth living," led to the "Socratic Method" of arriving at knowledge through asking questions. Socrates and his method of questioning gives to the history of Political Theory an irreverent and critical stance towards conventional wisdom and social pretense.

Perhaps the best representation of Socrates' life is Plato's dialogue, *The Apology*, which describes his trial in Athens on charges of heresy and corrupting the youth. This trial, and its conclusion in a death sentence, foreshadows the rest of Political Theory, where critical questioning and challenging of established authority often leads to State censorship and persecution. But Socrates' teachings in *The Apology* are important also for the fundamental themes they raise, often taken up by his student, Plato, in *The Republic*.

Socrates begins his defense in *The Apology* by saying how he is going to speak. How one speaks is essential to Classical Political Theory, because politics consists of reasoned speech and justice derives from the knowledge distilled through public deliberation. So, the integrity of speech is necessary to a just society. Socrates contrasts his simple, honest speech with the deceitful eloquence of his opponents, who were taught fine rhetoric by the Sophists.

> I do not know what effect my accusers have had upon you, gentlemen, but for my own part I was almost carried away by them; their arguments were so convincing. On the other hand, scarcely a word of what they said was true.
>
> I have not the slightest skill as a speaker—unless, of course, by a skillful speaker they mean one who speaks the truth....what you will hear will be a straightforward speech in the first words that occur to me, confident as I am in the justice of my cause....It would hardly be suitable, gentlemen, for a man of my age to address you in the artificial language of a schoolboy orator.[1]

Having said how he is going to address the Athenean jury, Socrates states *who* he is going to address, and breaks down his accusers into two categories: (1) past accusers and (2) present accusers. His past accusers are those who have been maligning him for years, influencing the present jurors in their youth.

> I mean the people who took hold of so many of you when you were children and tried to fill your minds with untrue accusations against me, saying 'There is a clever man called Socrates who has theories about the heavens and has investigated everything below the earth, and can make the weaker argument defeat the stronger.'[2]

For Socrates, these past accusers are the most dangerous, because they cannot be cross-examined and because they influenced adult Atheneans in their youth, when they were impressionable. This concern with the influences on young minds and their effects on adult citizens is an important Socratic theme developed by Plato in *The Republic*. Socrates implies, and Plato insists, that what children are exposed to will affect their adult character and beliefs, and therefore it is important to carefully screen what young people see and hear. This leads Plato's *Republic* to have an elaborate educational system that limits what children learn until they are ready.

So, Socrates' identification of two immediate problems with his trial (that past accusers cannot be answered and that present jurors' minds are already prejudiced against him) is an indictment of Athenean society and Greek justice. Having invalidated the legal process itself, Socrates proceeds to dismiss the two charges against him (heresy and corrupting the youth) as pretexts for a deeper attack on his philosophical activity.

---

1   Plato, *The Apology* in *The Last Days of Socrates*, translated by Hugh Tredennick (New York: Penguin, 1981), p. 45.
2   Plato, p. 46.

He explains that his philosophical pursuits-his habit of questioning others in search of truth, began when a friend informed him that the Oracle at Delphi said that Socrates is the wisest man in Greece. Puzzled by this statement, Socrates set about to disprove the Oracle's judgement by finding a man in Athens wiser than himself.

> After puzzling about it for some time, I set myself at last with considerable reluctance to check the truth of it in the following way. I went to interview a man with a high reputation for wisdom, because I felt that here if anywhere I should succeed in disproving the oracle and pointing out to my divine authority 'You said that I was the wisest of men, but here is a man who is wiser than I am.'

> Well, I gave a thorough examination to this person-I need not mention his name, but it was one of our politicians...and in conversation I formed the impression that although in many people's opinion, and especially in his own, he appeared to be wise, in fact he was not. Then when I began to try to show him that he only thought he was wise and was not really so, my efforts were resented both by him and by many of the other people present. However, I reflected as I walked away: 'Well, I am certainly wiser than this man.' It is only too likely that neither of us has any knowledge to boast of; but he thinks that he knows something which he does not know, whereas I am quite conscious of my ignorance. At any rate it seems that I am wiser than he is to this small extent, that I do not think that I know what I do not know.[3]

Thus, a humble appreciation of one's own ignorance and the continual search for truth becomes Socrates' definition of wisdom. And he does not stop with the politician. He questions reputed wise men in the arts, poetry and business, and finds them. all either ignorant of their own craft or knowledgeable in that area and therefore, presuming knowledge in all areas. And this discovery of ignorance and arrogance in many of Athens' most respected citizens does not make Socrates very popular.

> The effect of these investigations of mine, gentlemen, has been to arouse against me a great deal of hostility, and hostility of a particularly bitter and persistent kind....[4]

This resentment was compounded by the fact that several aristocratic young men had gotten in the habit of accompanying Socrates on his philosophical

---

3   Plato, p. 50.
4   Plato, p. 52.

quests and delighting in the humiliation of respectable elders in the community. Some of these young men even began imitating Socrates by critically questioning older citizens and revealing their ignorance. This, Socrates claims, becomes the basis of the charge of "corrupting the youth."

Socrates refutes this charge by questioning his chief accuser, Meletus, and revealing the contradictions in his accusation. His rebuttal is complex, but it goes something like this:

> Socrates: "Does anyone want to harm himself?"
>
> Meletus: "No."
>
> Socrates: "Do the people one associates with affect one, evil associates affecting one badly and good associates affecting one well?"
>
> Meletus: "Yes."
>
> Socrates: "When one corrupts one's associates does it make them better or worse?"
>
> Meletus: "Worse, of course."
>
> Socrates: "Did I corrupt my young associates intentionally or unintentionally?"
>
> Meletus: "Intentionally."

At this point, Socrates has tied Meletus up in a logical knot and is able to destroy his accusation of corrupting the youth.

> Why, Meletus, are you at your age so much wiser than I at mine? You have discovered that bad people always have a bad effect, and good people a good effect, upon their nearest neighbors; am I so hopelessly ignorant as not even to realize that by spoiling the character of one of my companions I shall run the risk of getting some harm from him? ...Either I have not a bad influence, or it is unintentional; so that in either case your accusation is false.[5]

This refutation of the charge of "corrupting the youth" with its emphasis on the effect of one's companions on one's own welfare, again, finds its way into Plato's political theory. Plato's *Republic* places authority in the philosopher king, who orders society so that each class of citizens associates with those who will reinforce their virtues, for the improvement of justice for all.

Socrates now refutes the second charge against him (heresy or impiety) in typical fashion. The charge includes two components: (1) that Socrates teaches

---

5   Plato, p. 56.

about supernatural activities and (2) that he does not believe in the gods. Again, Socrates refutes the charge by questioning Meletus and revealing contradictions in his own accusation. The interrogatory goes like this:

> Socrates: "If one teaches about human *activities* must he assume the existence of humans?"
>
> Meletus: "Yes."
>
> Socrates: "And, if one teaches about horses' activities, must he assume the existence of horses?"
>
> Meletus: "Yes."
>
> Socrates: "Then, if one teaches about supernatural activities, as you accuse me of doing, then one must assume the existence of supernatural beings, or gods, which makes your charge that I teach about supernatural activities but do not believe in gods illogical."[6]

By exposing the inconsistencies in Meletus' charges against him, Socrates reveals them for what they are: trumped-up charges disguising the true charge of his philosophical questioning that embarrasses Athens' leading citizens. What the court really wants is for Socrates to quit critically examining Athenean society and conventional wisdom. But, Socrates declares that he cannot stop his philosophical life because it is a duty to God. Furthermore, he sees it as good for Athens to be challenged in this way because, like a fat cow, it has become lazy and luxurious and needs a gadfly to rouse it. Still, Socrates admits that no society, especially a democracy, cares to be challenged and so seldom tolerates philosophical questioning.[7]

He was right. Socrates is found guilty by the Athenean court and Meletus suggests the death penalty. Socrates is permitted to offer an alternative punishment. He refuses to suggest the obvious alternatives of a fine or banishment or silence. Instead, he suggests that the state grant him a pension, so that he can continue his philosophical inquiries more comfortably. This, Socrates insists, is what he "deserves."

This infuriates the jury so that they vote the death penalty. Socrates' proposal that the philosopher be supported by society is dashed, until Plato revives the idea in *The Republic*. Socrates accepts the death sentence, but offers a prophesy to the Athenean court:

---

6   Plato, p. 58.
7   Plato, p. 64.

> As soon as I am dead, vengeance shall fall upon you with a punishment far more painful than your killing of me. You have brought about my death in the belief that through it you will be delivered from submitting your conduct to criticism; but I say that the result will be just the opposite. You will have more critics....[8]

> If you expect to stop denunciation of your wrong way of life by putting people to death, there is something amiss with your reasoning. This way of escape is neither possible nor credible; the best and easiest way is not to stop the mouths of others, but to make yourselves as good men as possible.[9]

This Socratic advice, which has been given to tyrants ever since, is followed by Socrates' forgiving his executioners and requesting that they show him "justice" by treating his sons as he treated them:

> I bear no grudge at all against those who condemned me and accuse me....However, I ask them to grant me one favor. When my sons grow up, gentlemen, if you think they are putting money or anything else before goodness, take your revenge by plaguing them as I plagued you; and if they fancy themselves for no reason, you must scold them just as I scolded you, for neglecting the important things and thinking that they are good for something when they are good for nothing. If you do this, I shall have had justice at your hands, both I myself and my children.[10]

This Socratic definition of justice as goodness through education and criticism is developed by his greatest student, Plato, in *The Republic*.

---

8   Plato, p. 73.
9   Plato, p. 74.
10 Plato, p. 76.

· 2 ·

Plato's Perfect Republic

Plato's *Republic* is the first great work in Political Theory. It raises the fundamental questions of Human Nature, Political Society and Social Ethics. Some consider Plato's *Republic* still the best book in the history of Political Theory, claiming that, like Scripture, all answers to political questions are within it, if only you know where to look. Whether or not that is true, Plato's work does provide the first systematic examination of the essential issues in Political Theory and attempts to formulate a definition of Justice. Plato's authoritarian "ideal" regime and his criticism of democracy has caused some, especially in the twentieth century, to blame Platonic philosophy for Fascism and Communism. Whether Plato is the greatest hero or the greatest villain of Political Theory remains a subject of debate.

Human Nature

Plato conceives of Human Nature or man's "soul" as containing three elements or dispositions: (1) the Philosophic, (2) the Spirited and (3) the Appetitive.

The Philosophic part of the soul is the desire and capacity for knowledge. Socrates obviously displayed this philosophic disposition in his ceaseless search for knowledge and his insatiable curiosity and questioning of others. The philosophic element requires capacities for listening and comprehending, critical reasoning and skillful communication.[1]

The Spirited part of human nature is that passionate impulse towards combat and victory. It loves the fight, the excitement of a conflict and the exhilaration of triumphing over one's opponent. In its fullest development, the Spirited soul is a warrior, or in modern America, a football player.

The Appetitive element of the soul is concerned with material things physical appetites for food, clothing, luxuries, etc. It likes things, possessions; it is a consumer. Broadly speaking, the Appetitive nature is interested in economics: the production, distribution and consumption of material goods. He is homo economicus or a businessman.

For Plato, each of these three elements is present in every person, though different dispositions are dominant in different individuals. Those whose personality is marked by an interest in acquiring knowledge, a curiosity about many things, and an unending search for truth have the Philosophic element dominant in their souls. Those who love struggle and conflict, who are continually striving to triumph over others, have the Spirited element dominant in their souls. And those who are primarily concerned with the comforts of life, with acquiring and enjoying material goods, have the Appetitive element dominant in their souls. For Plato, this distribution of dominant dispositions renders people essentially unequal. This difference among individuals on the basis of the Philosophic, the Spirited and the Appetitive elements in their souls, forms the basis for a natural class system in society.

Political Society

Corresponding to the three elements in the soul, for Plato, are three natural social classes: (1) the Philosophic or wise should rule, (2) the Spirited or courageous should defend, and (3) the Appetitive should produce.

For Plato, therefore, the State is merely the individual "writ large" and Justice concerns the *proper ordering* of elements within each. That Justice requires, first of all, the recognition of these different elements and the acceptance of *inequality* among individuals and *classes* in society. In Plato's time, as in our own, the notion that individuals are fundamentally unequal and that society must be

---

1 Plato, *The Republic*, translated by Allan Bloom (New York: Basic Books, 1968), pp. 164-167.

structured along strict class lines, was repugnant to many (especially the non-philosophic). Therefore, Plato devised a "noble lie" that would justify this natural order, which is known as The Myth of the Metals.[2] According to this myth, all humans were created inside the earth and their bodies were mixed with different metals: the Philosophic natures were mixed with Gold, the Spirited natures were mixed with Silver, and the Appetitive natures were mixed with Bronze. This myth, therefore, explained and justified the differentiation of individuals and classes, in terms comprehensible to common people. But there remains the problem of how you really determine those distinctions of character.

The discovery of which metal or disposition resides in each individual rests with Plato's elaborate educational system, which discerns the dominant element in each child and trains it accordingly. Because, Plato insists, the predominant element in each person is not hereditary—it is not passed on by one's parents. That means that Gold parents can have a Bronze child and Bronze parents can produce a Gold or Silver child, etc. So Plato's class system is not that of Medieval Europe, where your status was determined by your parents, and if they were peasants, you were a peasant. Rather, Plato's *Republic* has a kind of communism of children in which all parents give their children up to the state to be categorized and educated in the appropriate class.[3] Interestingly, Plato does not discriminate according to sex; both men and women can be Gold, Silver or Bronze.[4]

The goal of the education of each psychological disposition is the cultivation of its "virtue." The virtue of a thing is that quality or character that makes it function well. The virtue of a knife is sharpness—so that it can perform its function, cutting, well. For Plato, the virtue of the Philosophic element of the soul is Wisdom; the virtue of the Spirited element is Courage; and the virtue of the Appetitive element is Moderation, in both individual and state.[5]

Without the training of reason and accumulation of knowledge (Wisdom), the Philosophic disposition remains aimless, undisciplined curiosity. Without the training and discipline of Courage, the Spirited element is wild and dangerous. And, without the virtue of Moderation, the Appetitive element of the soul is grasping and greedy. Justice, therefore, resides in the proper ordering of individuals in appropriate classes and their education in the relevant virtue.

---

2   Plato, p. 94.
3   Plato, p. 101.
4   Plato, pp. 132–133.
5   Plato, p. 105.

The Philosophic element rules this just order because it alone, for Plato, knows the virtues of *all* classes of society; it knows its own virtue and those of others.[6] It is the only class that does so. The Philosophic ruler knows that its virtue is Wisdom, that the military's virtue is courage and that the businessperson's virtue is moderation. If the other classes of society ruled, they, who know only their own virtue, would impose it on everyone, which would be unjust. A military regime would expect all individuals and classes to conform to their virtues of courage, strength and honor. If the government were run by the business interests, it would treat the whole society as a corporation, looking only at production and consumption and measuring all endeavors according to a profitmotive. In such a society the only knowledge that would be valued would be knowledge of business; and the military would be turned into a corporation, with soldiers recruited with monetary incentives, rather than appeals to honor and glory.

Only the Philosopher knows the peculiar virtues of each class and gives them their "due," or what is necessary to educate and perform their function. For example, the soldier class must face the hardships of war and so must be trained to endure rough conditions and be fierce and disciplined. Given this function, it would be "unjust" to provide them with luxuries and a soft life, since it would not prepare them for their duty. Similarly, the business class must have knowledge of production, distribution and consumption, and carry on trade for a moderate profit. It would be "unjust" to expect them to be concerned with matters of honor or abstract philosophy.

Social Ethics

Justice, therefore, is "giving each his due."[7] The just society recognizes and educates each citizen's individual talents, according to the dominant element in their soul and orders these elements into coherent classes. The just individual knows and performs his or her task responsibly and respects others for their function and contribution to the good of the whole society. If providing soldiers with strict discipline and rough provisions seems unkind, Plato reminds us that it is not for their pleasure (which is an Appetitive value), but their function that the government must be concerned about.[8] It would be unjust to treat a busi-

---

6   Plato, p. 122.
7   Plato, p. 27.
8   Plato, p. 98.

nessperson with such stinginess, since they love property and are motivated by profit, but the Spirited element wants and needs honor and victory. Similarly, it would be inappropriate to subject the philosophic soul, which is delicate, to either the harsh rigors of the military or the materialism of the business world.

If only the Philosopher can know the different virtues of the different classes in society and therefore "give them their due," and establish justice, it is necessary for him to rule. As Plato asserts, in a famous remark:

> Unless the philosophers rule as kings or those now called kings...philosophize... there is no rest from ills for the cities....[9]

Revolution: The Degeneration of Regimes

But the philosopher does not rule as king. And even if he does, Plato shows, change is inevitable. In Book VIII of *The Republic*, Plato describes how revolutionary change occurs in a logical way, given the strengths and weaknesses of all regimes. According to Plato, each regime has a distinctive "virtue" or excellence appropriate to its ruling class, and a "vice" or deficiency, which brings forth a revolution.

For Plato, the force that drives this logical sequence of revolutions is the fact that each successive regime's virtue satisfies the deficiency in the former regime. So, for example, the best regime of an Aristocracy of Philosopher Kings contains the deficiency of lack of Honor, which is satisfied by the regime that overthrows it, the military Timocracy, which is the rule of the Spirited element of the soul, which imposes the rigors of army life on the entire society. Those rigors include asceticism or poverty—that lack of luxury and finery that characterizes the military. Eventually tiring of this impoverished life under the military, the people are drawn to the rule of the few wealthy or Oligarchy, which riches galore and extols gracious, opulent living. The wealthy Oligarchs are the first of the Appetitive regimes, where the economic part of the soul gains political ascendency. The problem with the wealthy Oligarchs is that they don't want to share their wealth and use political power to amass more and more money (such as through State Monopolies). This greed of the Oligarchy brings on the next regime, Democracy, whose creed of Equality promises to distribute the wealth of the few to the many. Democracy's other virtue is Freedom, by which is meant the individual freedom to pursue wealth without restrictions by the State. So,

---

9   Plato, p. 153.

Democracy's values of Equality and Freedom are an economic response to Oligarchic hoarding of wealth. But, Plato insists, the freedom of Democracy eventually becomes license and anarchy, as every individual pursues his or her own self-interest without limits to restrain naked avarice. Therefore, Freedom and Equality come to mean individual freedom to pursue material gain equally with all others, without regard for others. This is the triumph of the Appetitive element of the soul, which has finally imposed its standard of materialism on the entire society (but without the limit of moderation imposed by the Philosopher-King). The wild scramble for economic gain by all in society eventually leads to chaos and anarchy. Soon the turmoil of Democracy leads all to be in danger and deprivation and this causes a public outcry for "order." The regime that answers this cry and imposes order quickly is Tyranny. One strong leader comes to power promising to restore order and decency to society. But he does so by imposing his own will, destroying all opposition and eventually indulging only his own appetites. So, out of Democratic Freedom comes the Tyrant's Order; out of the greatest liberty comes the greatest slavery.

Plato's theory of revolution in which each successive regime satisfies the deficiency of the former regime, but brings a worse deficiency of its own, is instructive to a century known for its revolutions. Ironically, both the best and the worst States, Aristocracy and Tyranny, are one-man rule or monarchy. Both offer order in society, though the Aristocrat's is derived from the just and harmonious ordering of classes and the Tyrant's is his own will imposed with violence and brutality. The importance of this Platonic view is that the form of government is less significant than the character of the rulers: a monarchy can be the best or the worst regime. The quality of the rulers is more important than the quantity of those rulings.

Plato does not suggest what happens to a State that has reached the bottom of regimes, Tyranny. His own logic does not hint at whether or not the regime addressing the deficiency of Tyranny, Cruelty, would be Democracy (and on up the scale) or Aristocracy (and back down).

Plato's Critique of Democracy

Because Americans like to believe that they live in a democracy it might be useful to examine Plato's description of a Democratic Regime more carefully.

For Plato, Democracy emerges from the frustration of the majority with the concentrated wealth of the minority protected by an Oligarchic government. The Oligarchy constitutes the few very rich families who use political power to preserve and expand their wealth (such as through State monopolies). This excludes the masses of people from participating freely in commerce on an equal footing with the Oligarchs. Eventually, the gap between the enormous wealth and luxury of the few and the poverty and deprivation of the many causes a Democratic revolution. The battle-cry of a Democratic revolution is "Equality and Freedom," by which is meant equal access to wealth by the poor and freedom to pursue wealth unencumbered by the State. Once established, the Democratic regime treats all citizens equally ("Equality before the Law") and lifts restrictions on economic activity ("Free Enterprise").

Plato says that this egalitarian posture of the Democratic regime causes all kinds of people, especially the poor of other nations, to migrate to the Democracy, creating a rich variety of nationalities and diversity of cultures. And, all being treated equally, many view this Democracy as the fairest of regimes:

> Just like a many-colored cloak decorated in all hues, this regime, decorated with all dispositions, would also look fairest, and many...would judge this to be the fairest regime.[10]

However, this equality, established to better the masses, soon destroys them. For Plato, after all, people are unequal, with different dispositions dominating their souls. The effect of saying that all are equal is that the "inferior" dominate their "betters" and injustice ensues. Plato predicts that all subordinates will demand "liberation" from their "oppressors": children will rebel against the authority of their parents; the young will be disrespectful towards their elders; students will be insolent towards their teachers; the base, appetitive impulses of the soul will reject reasoned moderation and ridicule the philosophic. All pleasures will be considered equal and each individual will be free to indulge them.[11] If everything is the same, there exist no legitimate grounds for authority or standards for "better" or "worse." Eventually, this uncontrolled freedom and equality will erupt into chaos and anarchy and the limited state will have no basis for control.

The government of a democracy becomes increasingly ineffective, as it caters to the whims of the masses. Because politicians have to be elected by a diverse population, they appeal to the lowest common denominator—the base appetites of the people. Such a government cannot rule justly, for Plato, because it cannot

---

10   Plato, p. 235.
11   Plato, pp. 239–242.

distinguish among natural classes in society nor discipline them in their native talents.

Because of the chaos of Democratic society and the impotence of Democratic government, the people are increasingly inconvenienced by their own self indulgence and yearn for order. A strong leader emerges who promises order and decency and proceeds to impose it, through Tyranny.

· 3 ·

ARISTOTLE

Classical Democracy

Aristotle (384–322 B.C.) was a Greek philosopher who studied with Plato and wrote on a wide range of subjects, including biology, physics, logic, metaphysics, aesthetics, poetry, politics and ethics. As a student of Plato's Aristotle shared certain of the basic perspectives found in *The Republic* (the hierarchy of natures, justice as a relation or order among parts, the inevitability of social classes), but he also diverges from his master in several significant ways (the ideal regime, the dimensions of ethics and the causes of revolution, among others). Aristotle developed one of the most elegant and influential political theories, as evidenced not merely by Thomist Christianity, but also its effect on contemporary debates over man's social nature.

Human Nature

Aristotle conceived of man as naturally social and political: "by nature man is a political animal….[m]en have a natural desire for life in society…."[1] The source

---

1   Aristotle, *The Politics*, translated by T. A. Sinclair (Baltimore, Penguin, 1972), p. 114.

of that social nature, for Aristotle, is man's unique capacity for reasoned speech and moral choice. Reasoned speech distinguishes man from instinctually social species (such as bees), but, he claims, "the real difference between man and other animals is that humans alone have perception of good and evil, right and wrong, just and unjust."[2] These two faculties (reasoned speech and moral choice), for Aristotle, render man naturally social and political because neither can be developed or practiced in isolation. Man's unique characteristics make political society both possible and necessary for his full development.

Still, while man is born with the capacity for reasoned speech and moral choice, those faculties must be cultivated and refined if they are to reach their potential.

> Virtues are implanted in us neither by nature nor contrary to nature: we are by nature equipped with the ability to receive them, and habit brings this ability to completion and fulfillment...we are provided with the capacity (dynamis: potential) first, and display the activity (energia: actuality) afterward.[3]

And, for Aristotle, if those human faculties are not developed, it does not mean that man becomes simply like other animals; he falls below the level of beasts.

> As man is the best of all animals when he has reached his full development, so he is worst of all when divorced from law and morals.[4]

And, since the uniquely human qualities of reason, speech and ethics are also the political faculties, Aristotle attributes their proper development to a certain kind of political society.

Political Society

The best way to develop man's social and political faculties, for Aristotle, is through participation in the governance of small democratic communities, or the *polis*. This leads Aristotle to define citizenship as using one's unique human faculties through participation in the common life of the community, or politics.

---

2   Aristotle, pp. 28–29.
3   Aristotle, *Nicomachean Ethics*, translated by Martin Ostwald (Indianapolis, Bobbs-Merrill, 1962), p. 33.
4   Aristotle, *The Politics*, p. 29.

What effectively distinguishes the citizen from all others is his participation in Judgement and Authority, that is, holding office, legal, political, administrative.[5]

There are different kinds of citizens, but...a citizen in the fullest sense is one who has a share in the privileges of rule.[6]

So, by organizing a polity in which citizens participate directly in the governance of their shared community, Aristotle believes people will develop the individual's uniquely human abilities in reason, speech and ethics, and establish the most virtuous regime. For a true citizen is one "who has a share both in ruling and in being ruled with a view to a life that is in accordance with goodness."[7] The development of such an ideal state, however, requires Aristotle to discuss the family, economics and politics.

The Development of the State

Aristotle's description of the growth of the *polis* is influenced by his scientific studies, especially the growth of organic substances. Like a plant, the human individual and Community have a natural goal or end which their growth and development strives towards. This is known as Aristotle's teleological approach to nature—to look at the *telos* or full development of a thing, and define it from that standard, rather than at lesser stages of its development. Such a teleology looks at the stages of development and the potential for complete perfection. For example, the *telos* of an acorn is an oak tree. When Aristotle looks at a tiny acorn he sees its complete development into a great oak tree, but also recognizes the importance of environmental factors (rain, soil, sun) on whether the oak tree will become fully developed or stunted.

Man also has a *telos* which involves realizing the potential of his innate capacities for reasoned speech and ethical action. The environment necessary to develop that human *telos* involves not only material circumstances, but also human relationships in marriage, family and community. Each human association develops a part of the distinctly human *telos*, and together they develop the full person.[8]

---

5   Aristotle, *The Politics*, p. 102.
6   Aristotle, *The Politics*, p. 112.
7   Aristotle, *The Politics*, p. 112.
8   Aristotle, *The Politics*, p. 25.

> We arrive at the same conclusion if we approach the question from the standpoint of self-sufficiency. For the final and perfect good seems to be self-sufficient. However, we define something as self-sufficient not by reference to the "self" alone. We do not mean a man who lives his life in isolation, but a man who also lives with parents, children, a wife, and friends and fellow citizens generally, since man is by nature a social and political being.[9]

So, all of these human associations are necessary to the development of man's *telos*, but as some are parts of others, Aristotle calls them subordinate. The individual is encompassed by the family, as is the family by society and society by politics.

This is not to say that the individual or closer associations are insignificant for Aristotle, only that they are *part of* larger associations, on which to some extent they are dependent. It is in this sense that Aristotle says that the study of politics is "the master science,"[10] because the organization and activity of the state will determine the individual's development, the family structure, economic relations, etc.

That state emerges from lower associations. The first human association is the Household, which for Aristotle includes husband and wife, parents and children, and masters and servants. The second human association is the Village, which is a collection of related families. Both the Household and the Village serve economic purposes-providing man with the physical necessities of life. The highest human association, or State, is the first not based on blood relation or concerned with economic matters. The polis, or political community, is a collection of villages and allows citizens (which for Aristotle are male heads of households) to meet and discuss the common good, establishing a just society and developing their human faculties of reasoned speech and moral choice. Thus, while the Household takes care of man's needs for "mere life" or basic existence, the State nurtures his need for "the good life" or cultivation of his unique human faculties and *telos*.

The state crowns Aristotle's hierarchy because it completes man's teleological needs and orders the lower associations as reason orders passion.

> The final association, formed of several villages, is the city or state. For all practical purposes the process is now complete; self-sufficiency has been reached and so, it is now in a position to secure the good life.[11]

---

9   Aristotle, *Nicomachean Ethics*, p. 15.
10 Aristotle, *Nicomachean Ethics*, p. 4.
11 Aristotle, *The Politics*, pp. 27-28.

Thus, the completion of a human *telos* involves, for Aristotle, a kind of "self-sufficiency"; but it is not the kind associated with "rugged individualism" or solitary pleasure, but rather, having what you need to complete human development: family, friends, fellow-citizens, community. Such self-sufficiency includes the knowledge of and practice of social ethics.

Social Ethics

Aristotle conceives of two kinds of ethics: (1) functional virtue (*arete*) and (2) moral virtue (*ethike*). Functional virtue, as that of Plato's social classes, has to do with excellence in some worldly activity: the knife is virtuous because it is sharp and cuts well; the soldier is virtuous because he is courageous and fights well. Moral virtue consists of excellence in human relationships-to be good in one's relations with others, regardless of their function.[12] Since Aristotle's idea of functional ethics is essentially the same as Plato's we will focus on his conception of moral virtue, which is his original contribution.

To possess moral virtue for Aristotle a person must have a character which knows and habitually chooses "the Golden Mean" in his relations with others. Such a character is developed in the polis and through friendship and therefore is dependent on a kind of political education. Once developed, it enhances the community of which it is a part.

The Golden Mean is that action which resides between extremes in human behavior and leads the way to moral virtue. The Golden Mean is also "moderation" between the extremes of excess and deficiency.[13]

So, for Aristotle, moral virtue rests in the middle ground between two vices, excess and deficiency, making it possible to err in two ways but be good in just one.[14]

For example, the Golden Mean with respect to war is Courage, which resides between the excess of recklessness and the deficiency of cowardice. Courage takes the proper attitude towards fear-it is cautious about those things that are truly dangerous, but not afraid of everything. A deficiency of courage causes one to be fearful of many things unnecessarily and an excess of courage causes one to be reckless about real dangers.[15] It is just as bad to foolishly expose oneself and

---

12 Aristotle, *Nicomachean Ethics*, p. 33.
13 Aristotle, *Nicomachean Ethics*, p. 35, pp. 42-43.
14 Aristotle, *Nicomachean Ethics*, p. 42.
15 Aristotle, *Nicomachean Ethics*, p. 45.

one's comrades to genuine danger as it is to refuse to fight or desert one's comrades. The Golden Mean of Courage, therefore, is the proper stance of a soldier towards himself and his fellows in battle.

The Golden Mean with respect to money in human relationships is Generosity, while the deficiency is stinginess and the excess is extravagance.[16]

Generosity, for Aristotle, is giving money to others in the proper way and at the proper time. Interestingly, this virtue also includes taking or borrowing money from the proper sources. This virtue of generosity is not determined by the *amount* of money given, so a poor person giving a little can be more generous than a wealthy person giving more dollars, but less proportional to his wealth. Generosity, then, consists in sharing an appropriate amount of one's money with appropriate people at appropriate times. And the person of good character and moral excellence will know what and when is "appropriate." The vice of stinginess is refusing to give money when appropriate and the vice of extravagance is giving too much or to inappropriate recipients. Thus, the Golden Mean with respect to money is generosity, a moderate sharing of wealth and this is violated by both extreme grasping of one's money and extreme looseness with one's money.

The morally-correct attitude towards oneself, Aristotle calls Highmindedness. This is an accurate appreciation of one's accomplishments and expectation of recognition.[17] It is the Golden Mean between the excess of Vanity and the deficiency of Smallmindedness. If Highmindedness has what we today might call "a healthy self-image" or recognition of our strengths and weaknesses and rewards appropriate to them, Vanity has an inflated sense of one's importance and Smallmindedness has an inferiority complex. Both believing that one deserves nothing when one does, and believing that one deserves much more when one does not, are vices. Highmindedness is a healthy balance between the two, and therefore, the morally virtuous stance. And again, Aristotle would answer the question "how do I know?" with the statement, "the excellent character will just know."

The Golden Mean with respect to anger is Gentleness, with its deficiency being Apathy and its excess Short-temperedness. Gentleness, from which comes the concept of "the gentleman," is an unruffled, calm and dignified posture, in control of its emotions and only displaying anger at an appropriate object at an appropriate time. The excess of Short-temperedness is a bursting of emotion at

---

16 *Aristotle, Nicomachean Ethics*, pp. 84–88.
17 *Aristotle, Nicomachean Ethics*, pp. 95–97.

inappropriate times and at the wrong people. The deficiency of Apathy is the lack of angry expression even at appropriate times. However, Aristotle says that Short-temperedness is farther from the virtue of Gentleness than is Apathy.

With respect to human relations, Aristotle calls the Golden Mean "Friendliness" with the excess of Obsequiousness and the deficiency of Quarrelsomeness. A friendly person compliments the good and criticizes the bad. An obsequious person praises and flatters everyone and a quarrelsome person is critical of everything.

Finally, with respect to humor, Aristotle identifies the Golden Mean with Wit and its deficiency with Boorishness and its excess with Buffoonery. The witty person has a pleasant, clever sense of humor, making tactful jokes at appropriate times to appropriate people. The boor is humorless and takes everything (especially himself) seriously all the time. The buffoon makes rude jokes at any cost and is constantly displaying crude and vulgar levity.

For Aristotle, the ethical person knows and chooses the Golden Mean in all of his relations with others. This "moral virtue" flows from an excellent character that is developed and refined from a certain education. Attaining this character is part of man's *telos*. It is cultivated through participation in the politics of the small democratic polis and through certain kinds of friendship.

Friendship

Friendship, for Aristotle, contributes to the development of good character by correcting vices and giving examples of noble conduct. The Greek word *philia* is translated into "friendship," but it means more than our casual use of the term; philia signifies a particularly deep, strong association which may exist between friends, family members, colleagues, etc. We might call it a kind of "loving friendship."[18]

This friendship develops moral virtue, is indispensable to the human *telos* and serves all ages and conditions of men.

> Continuing in a sequence, the next subject which we shall have to discuss is friendship. For it is some sort of excellence or virtue, or involves virtue, and it is, moreover, most indispensable for life. No one would choose to live without friends, even if he had all other goods. Rich men and those who hold office and power are, above all others, regarded as requiring friends. For what good would their prosperity do them if it did not provide them with the opportunity for good works? And

---

18 *Aristotle, Nicomachean Ethics*, p. 214.

> the best works done and those which deserve the highest praise are those that are done to one's friends. How could prosperity be safeguarded and preserved without friends? The greater it is the greater are the risks it brings with it. Also, in poverty and all other kinds of misfortune men believe that their only refuge consists in their friends. Friends help young men avoid error; to older people they give the care and help needed to supplement the failing powers of action which infirmity brings in its train; and to those in their prime they give the opportunity to perform noble actions. (This is what is meant when men quote Homer's verse:) "When two go together...": friends enhance our ability to think and to act. Also, it seems that nature implants friendship in a parent for its offspring and in offspring for its parent, not only among men, but also among birds and most animals. (Not only members of the same family group but) also members of the same race feel it for one another, especially human beings, and that is why we praise men for being humanitarians or "lovers of their fellow men." Even when traveling abroad one can see how near and dear and friendly every man may be to another human being.[19]

The spirit of harmony between friends resembles the concord of just politics and can contribute to the state.

> Friendship also seems to hold states together, and lawgivers apparently devote more attention to it than to justice. For concord seems to be something similar to friendship, and concord is what they most strive to attain, while they do their best to expel faction, the enemy of concord.[20]

However, Aristotle explains that there are different kinds of friendship, as people establish associations for different reasons. The three motives for friendship are: (1) Use, (2) Pleasure and (3) Goodness. The friendship based on usefulness or utility is established because someone is useful to you—they may provide you with money, power, prestige, or some skill or possession. The friendship based on pleasure develops because one receives pleasure or good feelings from someone else (because they are attractice, sexy, funny, etc.). Both of these first two motives for friendship Aristotle calls "incidental," because they are based on some benefit the person brings to the other rather than on the person himself. Such friendships are easily dissolved, as the loss of the benefit extinguishes the motive for association.

> These three motives differ from one another in kind, and so do the corresponding types of affection and friendship. In other words, there are three kinds of

---

19   *Aristotle, Nicomachean Ethics*, pp. 214-215.
20   *Aristotle, Nicomachean Ethics*, p. 215.

friendship, corresponding in number to the objects worthy of affection. In each of these, the affection can be reciprocated so that the partner is aware of it, and the partners wish for each other's good in terms of the motive on which their affection is based. Now, when the motive of the affection is usefulness, the partners do not feel affection for one another *per se* but in terms of the good accruing to each from the other. The same is also true of those whose friendship is based on pleasure; we love witty people not for what they are, but for the pleasure they give us.

So we see that when the useful is the basis of affection, men love because of the good they get out of it, and when pleasure is the basis, for the pleasure they get out of it. In other words, the friend is loved not because he is a friend, but because he is useful or pleasant. Thus, these two kinds are friendship only incidentally, since the object of affection is not loved for being the kind of person he is, but for providing some good or pleasure. Consequently, such friendships are easily dissolved when the partners do not remain unchanged: the affection ceases as soon as one partner is no longer pleasant or useful to the other. Now, usefulness is not something permanent, but differs at different times. Accordingly, with the disappearance of the motive for being friends, the friendship, too, is dissolved, since the friendship owed its existence to these motives.[21]

True or "perfect" friendship, for Aristotle, is based on Goodness. The motive for the association is the other person's goodness and virtue and character. Such highminded friendship usually brings usefulness and pleasure with it, though of a higher kind, and it will endure even when usefulness and pleasure departs. Such perfect friendship between people of good character enhances the goodness of each participant.

Also, in loving a friend they love their own good. For when a good man becomes a friend he becomes a good to the person whose friend he is. Thus, each partner both loves his own good and makes an equal return in the good he wishes for his partner and in the pleasure he gives him. Now friendship is said to be equality, and both these qualities inhere especially in the relationship between good men.[22]

In this sense, again friendship resembles politics as Socrates' relation with the youth he "corrupted," both properly are concerned with the goodness of the other.

Friendship is present to the extent that men share something in common, for that is also the extent to which they share a view of what is just. And the proverb

---

21 Aristotle, *Nicomachean Ethics*, pp. 218-219.
22 Aristotle, *Nicomachean Ethics*, p. 224.

"friends hold in common what they have" is correct, for friendship consists in community.[23]

In such friendships, as in just communities, there will exist fewer complaints and quarrels because they are based on mutual good character and concern for the other. Friendships and states based on utility and pleasure will erupt into quarrels as soon as anyone sees a diminishing of usefulness or pleasure, as everyone will be looking after their own advantage.[24]

All of this: the good character that habitually chooses the Golden Mean; the excellence that establishes friendship based on goodness; and the justice that creates the harmony of perfect friendship in a community, produce human happiness.

Revolution

All regimes (even the best) are subject to change or revolution, according to Aristotle. He identifies the source of political change with the fundamental principles of the state. The basis of any constitution is its conceptions of equality and *justice*. In many cases, a state's definition of justice comes out of its conception of equality. For example, Aristotle contrasts the implications of two regimes' conceptions of equality.[25]

1. DEMOCRACY: Those equal in any respect are equal in all respects.

2. OLIGARCHY: Those unequal in any respect are unequal in all respects.

As with Plato, Aristotle sees Democracy as ruled by the principle of absolute equality based in the common desire for wealth. Because individuals have an equal desire for material things, they must be equal in all respects, and the state should treat them accordingly. An Oligarchy (the rule of the few rich), by contrast regards the wealthy as different from others in money and all other matters. The upperclass is not simply more affluent, it is more civilized, intelligent, skillful and interesting. In both regimes, Aristotle asserts, revolution occurs when the social reality diverges from the ruling regime's principle of equality or

---

23 Aristotle, *Nicomachean Ethics*, p. 231.
24 Aristotle, *Nicomachean Ethics*, pp. 240-241.
25 Aristotle, *The Politics*, p. 190.

(1)   When the state treats equals unequally or

(2)   When the state treats unequals equally.[26]

Both disjunctions of conceptions of equality with the social reality of equality can cause a revolution. An example of the first is the American Revolution. The American Colonists (Jefferson, Washington, Madison, etc.) regarded themselves and lived in material conditions as English citizens. When, therefore, the British Parliament treated them as second-class citizens, the Colonists rebelled. An example of the second situation is when the government, to benefit some disadvantaged minority, treats less qualified applicants (for education, employment, etc.) equally with more qualified applicants. This becomes an issue when affirmative action quotas caused some more qualified white men to be passed over for less qualified Blacks and women. The Whites, regarding themselves as unequal with the Blacks (by virtue of having superior qualifications), resented the state treating them "equally." However, since it is a minority of individuals in any society that are superior in wealth or talent, Aristotle insists that a Democracy which treats all citizens equally will be more stable and less likely to suffer a revolution.[27]

The Degeneration of Regimes

Aristotle differs with Plato on the logic of political change. First, he perceives multiple reasons for revolutions rather than simply a regime's prominent deficiency; and second, he sees the sequence of change differently from Plato.[28]

For Aristotle, if a regime changes, it is likely to retain its form but alter its substance. For example, he describes three types of regimes and the number of rulers that distinguishes them.

KINGSHIP	–	(rule of one)
ARISTOCRACY	–	(rule of few)
POLITY	–	(rule of many)

---

26 Aristotle, *The Politics*, p. 191.
27 Aristotle, *The Politics*, p. 192.
28 Aristotle, *The Politics*, pp. 192–197, p. 23.

In each of the above regimes, the government is considered "good" because, despite the number of rulers, it governs for the benefit of the whole society (rather than for the good of a part or for itself). A "bad" or degenerate regime is one that shares the same form, but rules for its own interest rather than that of the whole society.[29]

KINGSHIP	–	Tyranny
ARISTOCRACY	–	Oligarchy
POLITY	–	Democracy

The most stable regime, for Aristotle, is the "mixed regime," which combines the favorable attributes of each good regime and balances them together as the Founders of the American Constitution attempted to do:[30]

KINGSHIP	–	Presidency
ARISTOCRACY	–	Senate
POLITY	–	House of Representatives

The rulers bear the chief responsibility for the stability and justice of a regime and Aristotle advises them to follow these principles:

(1) remain loyal to the established Constitution (and its standards of equality);

(2) select governors with ability and skill;

(3) preserve the virtue appropriate to the regime (e.g., wealth in an oligarchy, freedom in a democracy, etc.).[31]

Finally, Aristotle, after Plato, sees Tyranny as the worst possible regime. It grows out of envy and resentment and maintains itself through these various forms of treachery:

(1) kill the best men

(2) outlaw social organizations

(3) discourage schools and learning

---

29 Aristotle, *The Politics*, p. 207.
30 Aristotle, *The Politics*, pp. 209–211.
31 Aristotle, *The Politics*, p. 213.

(4)   spy on citizens

(5)   promote internal strife and rivalries

(6)   keep the people busy and poor

(7)   make war with your neighbors

(8)   destroy serious, intelligent people.[32]

With the richness and insight of Aristotle's political theory, it is easy to understand how it has been so highly-regarded and influential in Ancient, Medieval and Contemporary times.

---

32   Aristotle, *The Politics*, pp. 225-227.

· 4 ·

Cicero

Roman Law and Empire

Cicero (106–43 B.C.) was a Roman lawyer and statesman. He was educated in the Greek Classics and intentionally applied the precepts of Plato and Aristotle to the realities of the Roman Empire. His books, *The Republic* and *The Laws*, were deliberate references to Plato's works of the same names. However, the realities of an expanding Roman Empire, which strained the traditional institutions of the Roman Republic and moved it increasingly towards monarchy, affect the manner in which Cicero adopts Greek political theory. His emphasis on military virtue and the rule of law (over other kinds of virtue and the quality of the rule of men) reflect the creative adaption of Greek thought to Roman exigencies. Cicero was attempting to retain traditional Roman virtue: patriotic republicanism and stoic duty, in an age when the Empire was becoming increasingly corrupt and decadent. Cicero was murdered by Antony's henchmen in 43 B.C., one year after the assassination of Caesar.

Human Nature

Cicero, after Aristotle, conceives of man as naturally social. But, unlike Aristotle, he does not identify this social and political nature in reasoned speech and moral choice, as much as in "a certain social spirit"[1] that produces a patriotic sense of duty to the whole nation. Virtue then is a kind of timocratic or military virtue, appropriate to a large empire.

> [Without active patriotism]...could [never] have delivered [our native land] from attack; nor could Gaius Duelius, Aulus Atilius, or Lucius Metellus have freed [Rome] from her fear of Carthage; nor could the two Scipios have extinguished with their blood the rising flames of the Second Punic War; nor, when it broke forth again with greater fury, could Quintus Maximus have reduced it to impotence or Marcus Marcelus have crushed it; nor could Publius Africanus have torn it from the gates of this city and driven it within the enemy's walls...I will content myself with asserting that Nature has implanted in the human race so great a need of virtue and so great a desire to defend the common safety that the strength thereof has conquered all the allurements of pleasure and ease.[2]

To the extent Cicero identifies man's social nature with Reason, it is not the "reasoned speech" of Aristotle, but reason embodied in Law-the universal standards of Roman Law that governed an Empire and relied less on excellent men than did the Greek *polis*.

> Therefore, since there is nothing better than reason, and since it exists both in man and God, the first common possession of man and God is reason. But those who have reason in common must also have right reason in common. And since right reason is Law, we must believe that men have Law also in common with the gods. Further, those who share Law must also share Justice; and those who share these are to be regarded as members of the same commonwealth.[3]

Political Society

So, the first prominent feature of Cicero's state is the "Rule of Law." Politics does not rely on Plato's philosopher-king or Aristotle's excellent men, but upon law.

---

1   Cicero, *The Republic and The Laws*, translated by Clinton Walker Keyes (Harvard University Press: 1928), excerpted in William Ebenstein, *Great Political Thinkers* (New York, Rinehart, 1957), p. 128.
2   Cicero, p. 125.
3   Cicero, p. 133.

For there is no principle enunciated by the philosophers—at least none that is just and honourable—that has not been discovered and established by those who have drawn up codes of law for States.[4]

This confidence in the just rule of law, without the education and ordering of the philosopher-king or the participation in ruling of the small, democratic *polis*, is uniquely Ciceronian, and represents well the Roman faith in universal law for establishing justice and governing a vast Empire. The European, and to a lesser extent Anglo-American, jurisprudence traditions, with their rules, regulations and precedent, grew out of this Roman Law.

Besides this emphasis on Reason as Law for the just political society, Cicero adopt Aristotle's advocacy of a mixed constitution to insure the stability of the state.

> ...[I consider] the best constitution for a State to be that which is a balanced combination of the three forms mentioned, kingship, aristocracy, and democracy, and does not irritate by punishment a rude and savage heart...[5]

Social Ethics

Reflecting his conception of virtue as the timocratic sense of duty, honor and self-sacrifice, Cicero identifies moral conduct with a kind of patriotic stoicism:

> ...yet I could not hesitate to expose myself to the severest storms, and, I might almost say, even to thunderbolts, for the sake of the safety of my fellow-citizens, and to secure, at the cost of my own personal danger, a quiet life for all the rest. For, in truth, our country has not given us birth and education without expecting to receive some sustenance, as it were, from us in return; nor has it been merely to serve our convenience that she has granted to our leisure a safe refuge and for our moments of repose a calm retreat; on the contrary, she has given us these advantages so that she may appropriate to her own use the greater and more important part of our courage, our talents, and our wisdom, leaving to us for our own private uses only so much as may be left after her needs have been satisfied.[6]

---

4 Cicero, p. 126.
5 Cicero, p. 132.
6 Cicero, p. 131.

He is especially concerned about the shift in Roman rulership from public spirited, patriotic men to the wealthy, as "the best" comes to mean private riches rather than military strength and a sense of public duty.

> ...If [the State] leaves [the selection of its rulers] to chance, it will be as quickly overturned as a ship whose pilot should be chosen by lot from among the passengers. But if a free people chooses the men to whom it is to entrust its fortunes, and, since it desires its own safety, chooses the best men, then certainly the safety of the State depends upon the wisdom of its best men, especially since Nature has provided not only that those men who are superior in virtue and in spirit should rule the weaker, but also that the weaker should be willing to obey the stronger.
>
> But they claim that this ideal form of State has been rejected on account of the false notions of men, who, through their ignorance of virtue—for just as virtue is possessed by only a few, so it can be distinguished and perceived by only a few—think that the best men are those who are rich, prosperous, or born of famous families. For when, on account of this mistaken notion of the common people, the State begins to be ruled by the riches, instead of the virtue, of a few men, these rulers tenaciously retain the title, though they do not possess the character of the "best." For riches, names, and power, when they lack wisdom and the knowledge of how to live and to rule over others, are full of dishonour and insolent pride, nor is there any more depraved type of State than that in which the richest are accounted the best.[7]

Of course, Cicero's hope for a revival of classical Republican virtue in Rome was disappointed. Rather than returning to the earlier military virtues of honor, duty and sacrifice for the good of the whole nation, the Roman Empire became increasingly opulent and decadent, turning over more and more of the hard work of defense to the tribes they had conquered, and which eventually conquered them. The change that Cicero was resisting was foretold in Plato's description of the shift from the Timocratic military regime to the Oligarchic regime of great wealth and luxury. But, the fall of the rich and decadent Roman Empire gave rise to the great critique of Classical virtue, by the first Christian political theorist, St. Augustine.

---

7   Cicero, p. 131.

· 5 ·

St. Augustine

Christian Political Theology

St. Augustine (354-430) was a Bishop of the Catholic Church in northern Africa and a leading theologian of his own time and ever since. Although his mother was Christian, St. Augustine went through Manichaen and Neo-Platonic phases before accepting the Faith. He is notable for his acceptance by both Roman Catholic and Protestant Churches. His book, *The City of God*, is the first systematic Christian political theory. It was written during the final days of the Roman Empire (the sacking of Rome by Alaric the Goth in 410), in part as a defense against the common charge that the Roman Empire fell because of the rise of Christianity.

Human Nature

St. Augustine presents the classically Christian view of man as both Fallen and Redeemed, sinful and saved. Humans are separated from God through disobedience to His will and law and redeemed through Christ's death and resurrection and God's Grace. Man, for St. Augustine, still wears the taint of Adam's Original Sin, as displayed in men's continuing wicked deeds.

> That the whole human race has been condemned in its first origin, this life itself, if life it is to be called, bears witness by the host of cruel ills with which it is filled. Is not this proved by the profound and dreadful ignorance which produces all the errors that enfold the children of Adam, and from which no man can be delivered without toil, pain, and fear? Is it not proved by his love of so many vain and hurtful things, which produces gnawing cares, disquiet, griefs, fears, wild joys, quarrels, law-suits, wars, treasons, angers, hatreds, deceit, flattery, fraud, theft, robbery, perfidy, pride, ambition, envy, murders, parricides, cruelty, ferocity, wickedness, luxury, insolence, impudence, shamelessness, fornications, adulteries, incests, and the numberless uncleannesses and unnatural acts of both sexes, which it is shameful so much as to mention; sacrileges, heresies, blasphemies, perjuries, oppression of the innocent, calumnies, plots, falsehoods, false witnessings, unrighteous judgments, violent deeds, plunderings, and innumerable other crimes that do not easily come to mind, but that never absent themselves from the actuality of human existence? These are indeed the crimes of wicked men, yet they spring from that root of error and misplaced love which is born with every son of Adam.[1]

Therefore, the Classical Greek view of human excellence and perfectability is a prideful illusion for St. Augustine. Until man recognizes that he is created by and dependent upon God, and acknowledges his falling away from God, and redemption in Christ, he will remain doomed to failure and pain. Christians can regain their Godly natures through Christ and thereby overcome total separation from God.

So, St. Augustine describes Human Nature as at once Godly and fleshly, fallen and redeemed, and he commends an ethic that recognizes the sinful side of humanity and the saving Grace of God.

Following Christ, who is perfect by being fully God and fully man, humans are supposed to resist evil in the world even to the point of death, with faith in the resurrection of Christ, that God redeems what the world destroys. This dual stance of being fallen and redeemed, requiring striving for perfection with the recognition of inevitable failure, St. Augustine recognizes as more difficult than either Classical perfection or skeptical pessimism. If, with the Greeks, one could strive for perfection (the excellent man) with the expectation of probable success, the striving would be tolerable. Or, if, with the skeptics, one felt no need to strive and could wallow in complacency, this also would be tolerable. But, to be required to strive for Christlike perfection, knowing that one will not succeed in this life, promises a life of tension and frustration. But, that is precisely,

---

1 St. Augustine, *The City of God*, excerpted in *The Political Writings of St. Augustine*, edited by Henry Paolucci (Chicago, Regnery Gateway, 1962), pp. 1-2.

for St. Augustine, what Christians are called to do: strive for the perfection of Christ, without the expectation of ever fully overcoming one's sinful nature and achieving perfection.

Political Society

That dilemma of the individual Christian's life corresponds to the political dilemma of "The Two Cities." Man's dual nature, for St. Augustine, leads him to be a citizen of two cities: The City of Man (representing all earthly regimes) and The City of God (representing the perfect justice and peace of God's Heavenly Kingdom).

The City of Man (all earthly governments regardless of form) is characterized by imperfect justice and peace, because of man's sinful nature, and extols the worldly values of power, wealth and prestige. The City of God is that eternal, perfect, peace and justice which extols the values of humility, poverty and love. At times, St. Augustine refers to the City of Man as "Babylon" or "Rome" and the City of God as "Jerusalem." The former is seen as the life of the flesh and is dominated by the love of man, while the latter is characterized by the life of the spirit and the love of God.

> And thus it has come to pass, that though there are very many and great nations all over the earth, whose rites and customs, speech, arms, and dress, are distinguished by marked differences, yet there are no more than two kinds of human society, which we may justly call two cities, according to the language of our Scriptures. The one consists of those who wish to live after the flesh, the other of those who wish to live after the spirit.[2]

> In enunciating this proposition of ours, then, that because some live according to the flesh and others according to the spirit there have arisen two diverse and conflicting cities, we might equally well have said, "because some live according to man, others according to God."[3]

> Two cities have been formed, therefore, by two loves: the earthly by love of self, even to contempt of God; the heavenly by love of God, even to contempt of self. The former glories in itself, the latter in the Lord. For the one seeks glory from men; but the greatest glory of the other is God, the witness of conscience. The one lifts up its head in its own glory; the other says to its God, "Thou art my glory,

---

2   St. Augustine, pp. 5-6.
3   St. Augustine, p. 7.

and the lifter up of mine head." In the one, the princes and the nations it subdues are ruled by the love of ruling; in the other, the princes and the subjects serve one another in love, the latter obeying, while the former take thought for all.[4]

So, unlike the Greek Classics, where the standard for goodness is man (Plato's philosopher-king, Aristotle's excellent man), Christianity places that standard above the world in a transcendent standard of perfection: God known through Jesus Christ.

The Church

The Church becomes essential in this new transcendent standard of goodness and justice. The Church, for St. Augustine, resides in the world as the representative of the City of God and preserver of its values of love and peace. Like Christ, therefore, the Church is "in, but not of," the world. It lives in the world of power and greed and sin, but preserves and presents the heavenly values of humility, love and redemption. And, also like Christ, the Church encourages the world to strive for Godly values and the realization of the Kingdom of Heaven. Thus, the Church is caught between the two cities, situated in both, but residing wholly in neither. This requires the Church to live as the individual Christian: acknowledging the fallen, sinful nature of the world, while encouraging it to strive for attainment of heavenly peace, love and justice. Again, as for the individual, it would be easier for the Church to do one or the other: either be completely *in* the world (administer the state, regulate the economy, etc.) or be entirely *not of* the world (concerned only with the afterlife, spiritual matters, worship, etc.). But St. Augustine insists that the Church must do both, being "in, but not of, the world." The Church does this by recognizing that the earthly city has a justice of its own (concerned with rights, property, privilege, etc.), but that since Christ's death and resurrection this is "comingled" with the heavenly justice and enhanced by it. The two cities remain dialectically related, separate but connected, as evidenced, for St. Augustine, by the fact that the most just states will be ruled by Christian men.

> But if we discard this definition of a people, and, assuming another, say that a people is an assemblage of reasonable beings bound together by a common agreement as to the objects of their love, then, in order to discover the character of any people, we have only to observe what they love. Yet whatever it loves, if only it is an

---

4   St. Augustine, p. 8.

assemblage of reasonable beings and not of beasts, and is bound together by an agreement as to the objects of love, it is reasonably called a people; and it will be a superior people in proportion as it is bound together by higher interests, inferior in proportion as it is bound together by lower. For, in general, the city of the ungodly, which did not obey the command of God that it should offer no sacrifice save to Him alone, and which, therefore, could not give to the soul its proper command over the body, nor to the reason its just authority over the vices, is void of true justice.

For though the soul may seem to rule the body admirably, and the reason the vices, if the soul and reason do not themselves obey God, as God has commanded them to serve Him, they have no proper authority over the body and the vices.[5]

Thus, in fact, true justice has no existence save in that republic whose founder and ruler is Christ, if at least any choose to call this a republic; and indeed we cannot deny that it is the people's weal. But if perchance this name, which has become familiar in other connections, be considered alien to our common parlance, we may at all events say that in this city is true justice; the city of which Holy Scripture says, "Glorious things are said of thee, O city of God."[6]

Social Ethics

Therefore, the Church should advise the State on matters of morality and justice. St. Augustine, as Bishop, was not bashful about exhorting worldly princes to follow the teaching of their Lord, as interpreted by the Church. In a letter to a Roman Magistrate, the Bishop claims that he would prefer that the Church never had to ask the assistance of the State, but that since all earthly power and authority comes from God, which the Church represents on earth, it is not inappropriate for it to do so.

I would indeed that the African Church were not placed in such trying circumstances as to need the aid of any earthly power. But since, as the apostle says, "there is no power but of God," it is unquestionable that, when by you the sincere sons of your Catholic Mother help is given to her, our help is in the name of the Lord, "who made heaven and earth." For oh, noble and deservedly honourable lord, and eminently praiseworthy son, who does not perceive that in the midst of so great calamities no small consolation has been bestowed upon us by God, in that you, such a man, and so devoted to the name of Christ, have been raised to the dignity

---

5 St. Augustine, pp. 42–43.
6 St. Augustine, p. 43.

of proconsul, so, that power allied with your goodwill may restrain the enemies of the Church from their wicked and sacrilegious attempts?[7]

This letter is a good example of St. Augustine's view of the proper relation of the Church of God in its relations with the State. In it, he seeks leniency for certain criminals who murdered some Catholic priests and, in the name of God's mercy, asks that they not be executed.

> Wherefore I write this letter to implore you by your faith in Christ, and by the mercy of Christ the Lord Himself, by no means to do this or permit it to be done. For although we might silently pass over the execution of criminals who may be regarded as brought up for trial not upon an accusation of ours, but by an indictment presented by those to whose vigilance the preservation of the public peace is entrusted, we do not wish to have the sufferings of the servants of God avenged by the infliction of precisely similar injuries in the way of retaliation. Not, of course, that we object to the removal from these wicked men of the liberty to perpetrate further crimes; but our desire is rather that justice be satisfied without the taking of their lives or the maiming of their bodies in any part, and that, by such coercive measures as may be in accordance with the laws, they be turned from their insane frenzy to the quietness of men in their sound judgment, or compelled to give up mischievous violence and betake themselves to some useful labour. This is indeed called a penal sentence; but who does not see that when a restraint is put upon the boldness of savage violence, and the remedies fitted to produce repentance are not withdrawn, this discipline should be called a benefit rather than vindictive punishment?
>
> Fulfill, Christian judge, the duty of an affectionate father; let your indignation against their crimes be tempered by considerations of humanity; be not provoked by the atrocity of their sinful deeds to gratify the passion of revenge, but rather be moved by the wounds which these deeds have inflicted on their own souls to exercise a desire to heal them.[8]

Elsewhere, St. Augustine insists that taking such advice of the Church is the duty of secular rules and that enhances the justice of The City of Man.

> If you recognize that you have received the virtues which you have, and if you return thanks to Him from whom you have received them, directing them to His service even in your secular office; if you rouse the men subject to your authority and lead them to worship God, both by the example of your own devout life and by

---

7   St. Augustine, p. 241.
8   St. Augustine, pp. 245–246.

your zeal for their welfare, whether you rule them by love or by fear if, in working for their greater security, you have no other aim than that they should thus attain to Him who will be their happiness-then yours will be true virtues, then they will be increased by the help of Him whose bounty lavished them on you, and they will be so perfected as to lead you without fail to that truly happy life which is no other than eternal life. In that life, evil will no longer have to be distinguished from good by the virtue of prudence, because there will be no evil there; adversity will not have to be borne with fortitude, because there will be nothing there but what we love; temperance will not be needed to curb our passions, because there will be no enticements to passion there; nor shall we have to practice justice by helping the poor out of our abundance, for there we shall find no poor and no needy.[9]

So, St. Augustine practiced what he saw as the proper function of the Church in the world: reproving earthly arrogance and power, and encouraging The City of Man to strive for the goodness and justice of The City of God. As he writes in another letter to a Roman ruler:

Be it yours to fix your thoughts on God, and to look to Christ, who has conferred on you so great blessings and endured for you so great sufferings. Those who desire to belong to His kingdom, and to live for ever happily with Him and under Him, love even their enemies, do good to them that hate them, and pray for those from whom they suffer persecution; and if, at any time, in the way of discipline they use irksome severity, yet they never lay aside the sincerest love. If these benefits, though earthly and transitory, are conferred on you by the Roman Empire,—for that empire itself is earthly, not heavenly, and cannot bestow what it has not in its power,—if, I say, benefits are conferred on you, return not evil for good; and if evil be inflicted on you, return not evil for evil. Which of these two has happened in your case I am unwilling to discuss, I am unable to judge. I speak to a Christian-return not either evil for good, nor evil for evil.[10]

By such advice, the Bishop implicitly asserts a hierarchy of authority with God at the top and the Church, as God's representative on earth, as above the State. This hierarchy is made explicit in one of St. Augustine's sermons:

Consider these several grades of human powers. If the magistrate enjoin any thing, must it not be done? Yet if his order be in opposition to the Proconsul, thou dost not surely despise the power, but choosest to obey a greater power. Nor in this case ought the less to be angry, if the greater be preferred. Again, if the Proconsul himself enjoin any thing, and the Emperor another thing, is there any doubt, that

---

9   St. Augustine, p. 271.
10 St. Augustine, pp. 287-288.

disregarding the former, we ought to obey the latter? So then if the Emperor enjoin one thing, and God another, what judge ye? Pay me tribute, submit thyself to my allegiance. Right, but not in an idol's temple. In an idol's temple He forbids it. Who forbids it? A greater Power. Pardon me then: thou threatenest a prison. He threateneth hell. Here must thou at once take to thee thy faith as a shield, whereby thou mayest be able to quench all the fiery darts of the enemy.[11]

This hierarchy of authority led the Medieval Catholic Church to exert tremendous power over earthly regimes and justifies its continued intervention in political affairs through Pastoral Letters, etc.

---

11 St. Augustine, pp. 311-312.

· 6 ·

St. Thomas Aquinas

Catholic Political Theory

St. Thomas Aquinas (1225–1274) is considered the greatest political theorist of the Middle Ages. He was born into a noble family in Italy, entered a Dominican order and studied at the University of Paris. At Paris, he came under the influence of the revived Classical studies, especially Aristotle. St. Thomas' philosophical writings blend traditional Christian theology and Aristotelian philosophy, and this is particularly evident in his political writings.

Human Nature

Man, for St. Thomas, is distinguished by his social and rational nature. Citing Aristotle, he makes this assertion:

> To be sure, the light of reason is placed by nature in every man, to guide him in his acts toward his end. Wherefore, if man were intended to live alone, as many animals do, he would require no other guide to his end. Each man would be a king unto himself, under God, the highest King, inasmuch as he would direct himself in his acts by the light of reason given him from on high. Yet it is natural for man,

more than for any other animal, to be a social and political animal, to live in a group.[1]

Man knows justice through his reasons and uses that knowledge to order his individual and social life. That knowledge, for St. Thomas, involves an understanding of the hierarchy of laws.

Political Society

The state, for St. Thomas, is merely a part of the universal empire of which God is the maker and ultimate ruler. Human law, therefore, is an inferior part of larger Divine Law. Justice resides in the proper placing of subordinate things within larger wholes and natural hierarchies. The kinds of law that form the natural authority of the Universe are (1) Divine Law, (2) Natural Law and (3) Human Law.

Divine Law is God's Eternal Law-the only perfect, unchanging universal law.

> ...a law is nothing else but a dictate of practical reason emanating from the ruler who governs a perfect community. Now it is evident, granted that the world is ruled by divine providence, as was stated in the First Part, that the whole community of the universe is governed by divine reason. Wherefore the very Idea of the government of things in God the Ruler of the universe has the nature of a law. And since the divine reason's conception of things is not subject to time but is eternal, according to Proverbs viii. 23, therefore it is that this kind of law must be called eternal.
>
> Reply Obj. I. Those things that are not in themselves exist with God, inasmuch as they are foreknown and preordained by Him, according to Romans iv. 17, "Who calls those things that are not, as those that are." Accordingly the eternal concept of the divine law bears the character of an eternal law in so far as it is ordained by God to the government of things foreknown by Him.[2]

Natural Law is that part of Divine Law that governs natural things: the planets, the seasons, animals, plants, etc. Only humans participate in the Divine Law by knowing Natural Law through their reason.

---

1   St. Thomas Aquinas, *On Kingship* in *The Political Ideas of St. Thomas Aquinas*, edited by Dino Bigongiari (New York, Hafner Press, Macmillan, 1975), p. 175.
2   St. Thomas Aquinas, *Summa Theologica* in *The Political Ideas of St. Thomas Aquinas*, edited by Dino Bigongiari (New York, 1975), pp. 12-13.

Wherefore, since all things subject to divine providence are ruled and measured by the eternal law, as was stated above (A. I), it is evident that all things partake somewhat of the eternal law, in so far as, namely, from its being imprinted on them, they derive their respective inclinations to their proper acts and ends. Now among all others the rational creature is subject to divine providence in the most excellent way, in so far as it partakes of a share of providence, by being provident both for itself and for others. Wherefore it has a share of the eternal reason, whereby it has a natural inclination to its proper act and end; and this participation of the eternal law in the rational creature is called the natural law. Hence the Psalmist after saying: "Offer up the sacrifice of justice," as though someone asked what the works of justice are, adds: "Many say, Who showeth us good things?" in answer to which question he says: "The light of Thy countenance, O Lord, is signed upon us"; thus implying that the light of natural reason, whereby we discern what is good and what is evil, which is the function of the natural law, is nothing else than an imprint on us of the divine light. It is therefore evident that the natural law is nothing else than the rational creature's participation of the eternal law.[3]

Human Law (or Positive Law) consists of particular expressions of Natural Law at specific times and places in human society. These are the laws that rulers make to apply the Divine Law through the Natural Law to particular social circumstances.

...it is from the precepts of the natural law, as from general and indemonstrable principles, that the human reason needs to proceed to the more particular determination of certain matters. These particular determinations, devised by human reason, are called human laws, provided the other essential conditions of law be observed, as stated above (Q. 90, AA. 2, 3, 4). Wherefore Cicero says in his Rhetoric that "justice has its source in nature; thence certain things came into custom by reason of their utility; afterward these things which emanated from nature and were approved by custom were sanctioned by fear and reverence for the law."

The human reason cannot have a full participation of the dictate of the divine reason but according to its own mode, and imperfectly. Consequently, as on the part of the speculative reason, by a natural participation of divine wisdom, there is in us the knowledge of certain general principles, but not proper knowledge of each single truth, such as that contained in the divine wisdom; so, too, on the part of the practical reason man has a natural participation of the eternal law, according to certain general principles, but not as regards the particular determinations

---

3 St. Thomas Aquinas, *Summa Theologica*, pp. 13–14.

of individual cases, which are, however, contained in the eternal law. [Hence the necessity that human reason proceed to certain particular sanctions of law.]⁴

Thus, St. Thomas Aquinas conceives of "superiority" of law in terms of comprehensiveness-Divine Law is more comprehensive and therefore encompasses Natural Law and Human Law. This emphasis on wholeness and self-sufficiency as a standard of superiority also derives from Aristotelian philosophy.

Human Law is subordinate to Natural Law and Divine Law because it is a *part of* these greater laws. Natural Law and Divine Law have authority over Human Law because they encompass and surpass it. And this, for St. Thomas Aquinas, is the basis of the supremacy of Church over State. The Church interprets Divine Law through Natural Law and the State makes Human Law with the advice of the Church.

St. Thomas also adopts Aristotle's teleological view of things understood according to their ends or purposes or goals, rather than by their incompleteness at any particular stage in their development. The goal of the State is, again, after Aristotle, to serve the common good by promoting virtue and punishing vice.

> ...Isidore says that "laws are enacted for no private profit, but for the common benefit of the citizens."
>
> I answer that, As stated above (A. I), the law belongs to that which is a principle of human acts, because it is their rule and measure. Now as reason is a principle of human acts, so in reason itself there is something which is the principle in respect of all the rest; wherefore to this principle chiefly and mainly law must needs be referred.—Now the first principle in practical matters, which are the object of the practical reason, is the last end; and the last end of human life is bliss or happiness, as stated above. Consequently, the law must needs regard principally the relationship to happiness. Moreover, since every part is ordained to the whole, as imperfect to perfect; and since one man is a part of the perfect community, the law must needs regard properly the relationship to universal happiness. Wherefore the Philosopher, in the above definition of legal matters, mentions both happiness and the body politic, for he says that we call those legal matters *just*, "which are adapted to produce and preserve happiness and its parts for the body politic," since the state is a perfect community, as he says in *Politics* i.I.⁵
>
> A law, properly speaking, regards first and foremost the order to the common good. Now to order anything to the common good belongs either to the whole people or to some one who is the vice-regent of the whole people. And therefore the

---

4   St. Thomas Aquinas, *Summa Theologica*, pp. 15-16.
5   St. Thomas Aquinas, *Summa Theologica*, p. 6.

making of a law belongs either to the whole people or to a public personage who has care of the whole people,....[6]

St. Thomas Aquinas conceives of "virtue" in both Aristotelian senses: *functional* virtue of different classes and talents in society and *moral* virtue of not harming but developing the excellence of others. The State's laws should address both kinds of virtue.

> ...a law is nothing else than a dictate of reason in the ruler by [which] his subjects are governed. Now the virtue of any sub ordinate thing consists in its being well subordinated to that by which it is regulated; thus we see that the virtue of the irascible and concupiscible faculties consists in their being obedient to reason; and accordingly "the virtue of every subject consists in his being well subjected to his ruler," as the Philosopher says. But every law aims at being obeyed by those who are subject to it. Consequently it is evident that the proper effect of law is to lead its subjects to their proper virtue; and since virtue is "that which makes its subject good," it follows that the proper effect of law is to make those to whom it is given good, either simply or in some particular respect. For if the intention of the lawgiver is fixed on true good, which is the common good regulated according to divine justice, it follows that the effect of the law is to make men good simply.
>
> ...Secondly, it belongs to the notion of human law to be ordained to the common good of the state. In this respect human law may be divided according to the different kinds of men who work in a special way for the common good: e.g., priests, by praying to God for the people; princes, by governing the people; soldiers, by fighting for the safety of the people. Wherefore certain special kinds of law are adapted to these men.[7]
>
> ...Isidore says: "Laws were made that in fear thereof human audacity might be held in check, that innocence might be safeguarded in the midst of wickedness, and that the dread of punishment might prevent the wicked from doing harm." But these things are most necessary to mankind. Therefore it was necessary that human laws should be made....
>
> ...man has a natural aptitude for virtue, but the perfection of virtue must be acquired by man by means of some kind of training. Thus we observe that man is helped by industry in his necessities, for instance, in food and clothing. Certain beginnings of these he has from nature, viz., his reason and his hands, but he has not the full complement, as other animals have to whom nature has given sufficiency of clothing and food. Now it is difficult to see how man could suffice for

---

6   St. Thomas Aquinas, *Summa Theologica*, p. 8.
7   St. Thomas Aquinas, *Summa Theologica*, pp. 25, 63.

himself in the matter of this training, since the perfection of virtue consists chiefly in withdrawing man from undue pleasures, to which above all man is inclined, and especially the young, who are more capable of being trained. Consequently a man needs to receive this training from another, whereby to arrive at the perfection of virtue. And as to those young people who are inclined to acts of virtue, by their good natural disposition, or by custom, or rather by the gift of God, paternal training suffices, which is by admonitions. But since some are found to be depraved and prone to vice, and not easily amenable to words, it was necessary for such to be restrained from evil by force and fear, in order that, at least, they might desist from evil-doing and leave others in peace, and that they themselves, by being habituated in this way, might be brought to do willingly what hitherto they did from fear, and thus become virtuous. Now this kind of training which compels through fear of punishment is the discipline of laws. Therefore, in order that man might have peace and virtue, it was necessary for laws to be framed, for, as the Philosopher says, "as man is the most noble of animals if he be perfect in virtue, so is he the lowest of all if he be severed from law and righteousness";...[8]

However, for Human Law to fulfill these purposes, it must have reference to Natural Law and Divine Law; and the State must seek the guidance of the Church. The higher laws will inform lawmakers of the natural and divine limits and potential of humankind. And, if the lower Human Law should conflict with the higher laws, the higher should prevail. St. Thomas gives two examples of this potential conflict of laws which illustrate their proper resolution; one has to do with property, the other with obedience.

Human Law protects the right to private property and St. Thomas Aquinas explains the several good purposes that property serves.

...it is lawful for man to possess property. Moreover this is necessary to human life for three reasons. First, because every man is more careful to procure what is for himself alone than that which is common to many or to all; since each one would shirk the labor and leave to another that which concerns the community, as happens where there is a great number of servants. Secondly, because human affairs are conducted in more orderly fashion if each man is charged with taking care of some particular thing himself, whereas there would be confusion if everyone had to look after any one thing indeterminately. Thirdly, because a more peaceful state is insured to man if each one is contented with his own. Hence it is to be observed that quarrels arise more frequently where there is no division of the things possessed.[9]

---

8   St. Thomas Aquinas, *Summa Theologica*, p. 56.
9   St. Thomas Aquinas, *Summa Theologica*, p. 130.

But, these advantages of private property derive from the God-given purpose of material things, the sustenance of human beings and so the wealthy should practice good stewardship and share with the needy.

> The second thing that is competent to man with regard to external things is their use. In this respect man ought to possess external things, not as his own, but as common, so that, to wit, he is ready to communicate them to others in their need. Hence the Apostle says: "Charge the rich of this world...to give easily, to communicate to others," etc....
>
> A man would not act unlawfully if by going beforehand to the play he prepared the way for others, but he acts unlawfully if by doing so he hinders others from going. In like manner a rich man does not act unlawfully if he anticipates someone in taking possession of something which at first was common property and gives others a share, but he sins if he excludes others indiscriminately from using it. Hence Basil says: "Why are you rich while another is poor, unless it be that you may have the merit of a good stewardship and he the reward of patience?"[10]

Similarly, if private property and the laws that protect it circumvent the Godly purpose of material things (to sustain human life) it becomes "lawful" for the poor to steal to prevent starvation. Divine Law overrules Human Law.

> Things which are of human right cannot derogate from natural right or divine right. Now, according to the natural order established by divine providence, inferior things are ordained for the purpose of succoring man's needs by their means. Wherefore the division and appropriation of things which are based on human law do not preclude the fact that man's needs have to be remedied by means of these very things. Hence whatever certain people have in superabundance is due, by natural law, to the purpose of succoring the poor. For this reason Ambrose says, and his words are embodied in the *Decretals*: "It is the hungry man's bread that you withhold, the naked man's cloak that you store away, the money that you bury in the earth is the price of the poor man's ransom and freedom."
>
> Since, however, there are many who are in need, while it is impossible for all to be succored by means of the same thing, each one is entrusted with the stewardship of his own things, so that out of them he may come to the aid of those who are in need. Nevertheless, if the need be so manifest and urgent that it is evident that the present need must be remedied by whatever means be at hand (for instance when a person is in some imminent danger, and there is no other possible remedy), then it

---

10 St. Thomas Aquinas, *Summa Theologica*, p. 130.

> is lawful for a man to succor his own need by means of another's property, by taking it either openly or secretly; nor is this, properly speaking, theft or robbery.[11]

Under such circumstances, the Divine Law of worldly wealth serving human need overrides the Human Law protecting accumulated property.

Likewise, the different levels of law ordain different standards of obedience. Citing St. Augustine, Aquinas outlines the requirements of obedience to higher authorities.

> Just as the actions of natural things proceed from natural powers, so do human actions proceed from the human will. In natural things it behooved the higher to move the lower to their actions by the excellence of the natural power bestowed on them by God; and so in human affairs also the higher must move the lower by their will in virtue of a divinely established authority. Now to move by reason and will is to command. Wherefore just as in virtue of the divinely established natural order the lower natural things need to be subject to the movement of the higher, so too in human affairs, in virtue of the order of natural and divine law, inferiors are bound to obey their superiors.[12]

> For as a gloss says on Romans xiii. 2, "They that resist the power, resist the ordinance of God. If a commissioner issue an order, are you to comply if it is contrary to the bidding of the proconsul? Again if the proconsul command one thing and the emperor another, will you hesitate to disregard the former and serve the latter? Therefore if the emperor commands one thing and God another, you must disregard the former and obey God." Secondly, a subject is not bound to obey his superior if the latter command him to do something wherein he is not subject to him. For Seneca says: "It is wrong to suppose that slavery falls upon the whole man; for the better part of him is excepted. His body is subjected and assigned to his master, but his soul is his own." Consequently in matters touching the internal movement of the will man is not bound to obey his fellow man, but God alone.[13]

Here we see the similarity between St. Augustine's City of God and St. Thomas Aquinas' Divine Law, both providing a measure and a check on The City of Man and Human Law, and both placing the Church above the State in ultimate authority.

---

11 St. Thomas Aquinas, *Summa Theologica*, p. 138.
12 St. Thomas Aquinas, *Summa Theologica*, p. 160.
13 St. Thomas Aquinas, *Summa Theologica*, p. 170.

Kingship

St. Thomas Aquinas is frequently regarded as the philosopher of the Middle Ages and is sometimes criticized for enshrining Monarchy as the only Godly form of government. Modern democratic thinkers assaulted the Catholic Church in their assault on Medieval institutions, especially Monarchy. For example, the French Revolution attacked the King and the Church as one entity.

Actually, St. Thomas, after Aristotle, categorized political regimes according to "just" (those that served the common good) and "unjust" (those that served their own interest) regimes, and detailed the several just forms of government.

> Two points are to be observed concerning the right ordering of rulers in a state or nation. One is that all should take some share in the government, for this form of constitution ensures peace among the people, commends itself to all, and is most enduring, as stated in *Politics* ii. 6. [The other point is one which has to do with the kind of regime, or, in other words, with the forms of government. Of these there are indeed several, as the Philosopher says, but the best ones are two, viz., the *kingdom*, in which one man rules on the strength of his virtue (prudence), and *aristocracy*, that is, the rule of the best, in which few govern, again on the strength of their virtue. Accordingly, the best form of government is to be found in a city or in a kingdom in which one man is placed at the head to rule over all because of the pre-eminence of his virtue, and under him a certain number of men have governing power also on the strength of their virtue]; and yet a government of this kind is shared by all, both because all are eligible to govern and because the rulers are chosen by all. For this is the best form of polity, being partly kingdom, since there is one at the head of all; partly aristocracy, in so far as a number of persons are set in authority; partly democracy, i.e., government by the people, in so far as the rulers can be chosen from the people and the people have the right to choose their rulers.[14]

Still, St. Thomas did seem to favor kingship and justifies it as the best regime with this logic:

> The government should serve the interest of the whole.
> The whole is a single entity.
> Monarchy is a single entity.
> Therefore, Monarchy can serve the whole interest most effectively.

---

14 St. Thomas Aquinas, *Summa Theologica*, p. 188.

This question may be considered first from the viewpoint of the purpose of government. The aim of any ruler should be directed toward securing the welfare of that which he under takes to rule. The duty of the pilot, for instance, is to preserve his ship amidst the perils of the sea and to bring it unharmed to the port of safety. Now the welfare and safety of a multitude formed into a society lies in the preservation of its unity, which is called peace. If this is removed, the benefit of social life is lost and, moreover, the multitude in its disagreement becomes a burden to itself. The chief concern of the ruler of a multitude, therefore, is to procure the unity of peace. It is not even legitimate for him to deliberate whether he shall establish peace in the multitude subject to him, just as a physician does not deliberate whether he shall heal the sick man encharged to him, for no one should deliberate about an end which he is obliged to seek, but only about the means to attain that end. Wherefore the Apostle, having commended the unity of the faithful people, says: "Be ye careful to keep the unity of the spirit in the bond of peace." Thus, the more efficacious a government is in keeping the unity of peace, the more useful it will be. For we call that more useful which leads more directly to the end. Now it is manifest that what is itself one can more efficaciously bring about unity than several—just as the most efficacious cause of heat is that which is by its nature hot. Therefore the rule of one man is more useful than the rule of many.[15]

Elsewhere, St. Thomas argues that since one God rules the universe, one man should rule the realm. In any case, the Christian King should rule for the common good and rely on the Church for guidance. For, just as a just king is the best ruler, an unjust king, or tyrant, is the worst ruler.

Further, a united force is more efficacious in producing its effect than a force which is scattered or divided. Many persons together can pull a load which could not be pulled by each one taking his part separately and acting individually. Therefore, just as it is more useful for a force operating for a good to be more united, in order that it may work good more effectively, so a force operating for evil is more harmful when it is one than when it is divided. Now, the power of one who rules unjustly works to the detriment of the multitude, in that he diverts the common good of the multitude to his own benefit. Therefore, for the same reason that, in a just government, the government is better in proportion as the ruling power is one—thus monarchy is better than aristocracy, and aristocracy better than polity—so the contrary will be true of an unjust government, namely, that the ruling power will be more harmful in proportion as it is more unitary. Consequently, tyranny is more harmful than oligarchy and oligarchy more harmful than democracy.[16]

---

15 St. Thomas Aquinas, *On Kingship*, pp. 179-180.
16 St. Thomas Aquinas, *On Kingship*, pp. 181-182.

Danger thus lurks on either side. Either men are held by the fear of a tyrant and they miss the opportunity of having that very best government which is kingship, or they want a king and the kingly power turns into tyrannical wickedness.[17]

Social Ethics

Thomist social ethics reflect the different kinds of law and their hierarchical relationship. Justice is the proper ordering of superior and inferior laws, virtues and classes. For Medieval Europe, this meant conforming to one's hereditary class obligations and privileges; and for the Roman Catholic Church, it means the hierarchy of ecclesiastical offices. Ethical conduct is that which rein forces that natural hierarchy and unethical behavior is that which challenges or destroys that hierarchy. In a radically democratic, egalitarian Modern age, where all are considered equal and any suggestion of "superiority" is taken as an affront to the people's rights, this conception of justice is often regarded, correctly or not, as reactionary.

---

17 St. Thomas Aquinas, On Kingship, p. 186.

· 7 ·

MACHIAVELLI

Power Politics

Niccolo Machiavelli (1469-1527), affectionately known as "Old Nick" (a traditional neologism for Satan), lived in Florence, Italy, and worked as a minor public official. He travelled widely on diplomatic missions, observing the politics of many petty Italian states. When a new regime took over in Florence, Machiavelli was forced into exile and spent the rest of his life isolated on a small farm scheming to regain political favor and a position in the Florentine government. His book, *The Prince*, was written during this time and dedicated to Lorenzo di Medici, the new ruler of Florence.

Machiavelli is considered the prince of Modern politics (if not the Prince of Darkness) because of his emphasis on power. The Ancients were concerned with wisdom and virtue, the Medieval theorists with God and Christian ideals, but Modernity, launched by the Renaissance, reduces politics and ethics to force and expediency. Machiavelli's *Prince* is a handbook for getting and keeping power. All other considerations are viewed through this goal, which is regarded as "realism." But to be a true "Machiavellian," one has to be more than just powerhungry; one must be sufficiently devious to *appear* to be virtuous while actually grasping more and more power. This deceit of appearing good, while in reality being ruthless in the pursuit and use of power, is the center of Machiavellian thought.

Human Nature

Machiavelli does not have a very positive view of mankind. He does not dwell, with Aristotle, on the excellent man, nor does he share St. Thomas Aquinas' faith in man's reasoned appreciation of Divine Law. The *reality* of human nature, for Machiavelli, is a grasping, greedy being always concerned with material things and ever dissatisfied with what he's got.

> It was a saying of ancient writers, that men afflict themselves in evil, and become weary of the good, and that both these dispositions produce the same effects. For when men are no longer obliged to fight from necessity, they fight from ambition, which passion is so powerful in the hearts of men that it never leaves them, no matter to what height they may rise. The reason of this is that nature has created men so that they desire everything, but are unable to attain it; desire being thus always greater than the faculty of acquiring, discontent with what they have and dissatisfaction with themselves result from it.[1]

This is a reality that any ruler must acknowledge. So, Machiavelli's handbook for rulers, *The Prince*, insists on not looking at ideal regimes (like Plato's *Republic*) or ideal men (like Aristotle's *telos* or St. Augustine's Christian), but at real men and states with all their greed, ambition and treachery. Only this, Machiavelli claims, will provide a useful political theory.

> ...my intention being to write something of use to those who understand, it appears to me more proper to go to the real truth of the matter than to its imagination; and many have imagined republics and principalities which have never been seen or known to exist in reality; for how we live is so far removed from how we ought to live, that he who abandons what is done for what ought to be done, will rather learn to bring about his own ruin than his preservation. A man who wishes to make a profession of goodness in everything must necessarily come to grief among so many who are not good. Therefore it is necessary for a prince, who wishes to maintain himself, to learn how not to be good, and to use this knowledge and not use it, according to the necessity of the case.[2]

So, unlike St. Augustine, who acknowledges man's sinful nature, but believes in his potential redemption and goodness through Christ, Machiavelli

---

1 Niccolo Machiavelli, *The Prince and the Discourses*, translated by Luigi Ricci (New York, Random House, 1950), p. 208.
2 Machiavelli, p. 56.

sees human nature as wholly evil and occasional expressions of benevolence as inexplicable.

> ...whoever desires to found a state and give it laws, must start with assuming that all men are bad and ever ready to display their vicious nature, whenever they may find occasion for it. If their evil disposition remains concealed for a time, it must be attributed to some unknown reason;....[3]

From this point of view, Machiavelli insists that rulers should possess only those "good" qualities that enhance their power and ability to deal with the essential wickedness of men.

> ...all men, and especially princes, who are placed at a greater height, are reputed for certain qualities which bring them either praise or blame. Thus one is considered liberal, another *misero* or miserly (using a Tuscan term, seeing that *avaro* with us still means one who is rapaciously acquisitive and *misero* one who makes grudging use of his own); one a free giver, another rapacious; one cruel, another merciful; one a breaker of his word, another trustworthy; one effeminate and pusillanimous, another fierce and high-spirited; one humane, another haughty; one lascivious, another chaste; one frank, another astute; one hard, another easy; one serious, another frivolous; one religious, another an unbeliever, and so on. I know that every one will admit that it would be highly praiseworthy in a prince to possess all the above-named qualities that are reputed good, but as they cannot all be possessed or observed, human conditions not permitting of it, it is necessary that he should be prudent enough to avoid the scandal of those vices which would lose him the state, and guard himself if possible against those which will not lose it him, but if not able to, he can indulge them with less scruple. And yet he must not mind incurring the scandal of those vices, without which it would be difficult to save the state, for if one considers well, it will be found that some things which seem virtues would, if followed, lead to one's ruin, and some others which appear vices result in one's greater security and well being.[4]

Another quality of rulers which enhances the stability of the state and "one's greater security and wellbeing," is the ability to be feared rather than loved. Given men's essentially wicked nature, their bonds of affection are much weaker than their desire for personal safety, and therefore, a wise prince wants his subjects to fear rather than love him.

---

3   Machiavelli, p. 117.
4   Machiavelli, pp. 56-57.

From this arises the question whether it is better to be loved more than feared, or feared more than loved. The reply is, that one ought to be both feared and loved, but as it is difficult for the two to go together, it is much safer to be feared than loved, if one of the two has to be wanting. For it may be said of men in general that they are ungrateful, voluble, dissemblers, anxious to avoid danger, and covetous of gain; as long as you benefit them, they are entirely yours; they offer you their blood, their goods, their life, and their children, as I have before said, when the necessity is remote; but when it approaches, they revolt. And the prince who has relied solely on their words, without making other preparations, is ruined; for the friendship which is gained by purchase and not through grandeur and nobility of spirit is bought but not secured, and at a pinch is not to be expended in your service. And men have less scruple in offending one who makes himself loved than one who makes himself feared; for love is held by a chain of obligation which, men being selfish, is broken whenever it serves their purpose; but fear is maintained by a dread of punishment which never fails.[5]

Thus, Machiavelli's conception of human nature as evil and vicious produces a general view of politics as ruthless and treacherous and of "wise" rulers acknowledging both.

Political Society

Machiavelli's discussion of specific political societies is restricted to two kinds of regimes, Monarchy and republics, and to how a new Prince can acquire and retain power in those regimes. Throughout his discussion, he remains "practical" about the "realities" of mankind and power.

Monarchies, Machiavelli tells us, can be either old (hereditary) or new. The hereditary monarchy has the stability of tradition and the conquering Prince will immediately face two sets of enemies: (1) those who benefitted from the old regime and (2) the supporters of the new Prince who do not get what they want. Each must be dealt with swiftly and effectively.

In the conquest of a foreign province, the new Prince will face yet other problems. Foreign provinces may be culturally distinct from the new Prince and may have a powerful nobility.[6] In such cases, Machiavelli advises, the new Prince can go live in the new province and rule directly or settle another people in the conquered area to rule it, or kill all the old nobility and appoint his own, beholden to him. In every instance, the Prince must look to expediency,

---

5   Machiavelli, p. 61.
6   Machiavelli, pp. 8-9, p. 15.

to doing whatever is necessary for acquiring and retaining control. The only ethics that are relevant are those which enhance those qualities. He advises rulers to adopt the semblance of old social values and forms while radically changing them.

> He who desires or attempts to reform the government of a state, and wishes to have it accepted and capable of maintaining itself to the satisfaction of everybody, must at least retain the semblance of the old forms; so that it may seem to the people that there has been no change in the institutions, even though in fact they are entirely different from the old ones. For the great majority of mankind are satisfied with appearances, as though they were realities, and are often even more influenced by the things that seem than by those that are. The Romans understood this well, and for that reason, when they first recovered their liberty, and had created two Consuls in place of a king, they would not allow these more than twelve lictors, so as not to exceed the number that had served the king. Besides this, the Romans were accustomed to an annual sacrifice that could only be performed by the king in person; and as they did not wish that the people, in consequence of the absence of the king, should have occasion to regret the loss of any of their old customs, they created a special chief for that ceremony, whom they called the king of the sacrifice, and placed him under their high priest; so that the people enjoyed these annual sacrificial ceremonies, and had no pretext, from the want of them, for desiring the restoration of the kings. And this rule should be observed by all who wish to abolish an existing system of government in any state, and introduce a new and more liberal one. For as all novelties excite the minds of men, it is important to retain in such innovations as much as possible the previously existing forms.[7]

For Machiavelli, deceiving the people in this way is quite laudable and greatly enhances the Prince's ability to get what he wants. Another good way to manipulate the people is to offer worse candidates along with the better to keep incompetent leaders from advancing.

> When the Roman Senate apprehended lest the Tribunes with consular powers should be taken from amongst the plebeians, they adopted one of the two following methods: either they caused the most distinguished and influential men of Rome to become candidates, or by suitable means they bribed some of the most sordid and ignoble to come forward as candidates at the same time with the better quality of plebeians, who usually asked for these offices. This latter course caused the people to be ashamed of bestowing them upon such candidates, and the former course made them ashamed to refuse them to such honorable citizens. All of

---

7   Machiavelli, pp. 182–183.

which corroborates what I have maintained in the preceding chapter, that in general matters the people are apt to deceive themselves, but rarely in particulars.[8]

However, in addition to a clever Prince, a stable regime will also need means (legal or personal) to revive and celebrate its Founding principles (such as the Supreme Court rulings interpreting the U.S. Constitution and the Bicentennial festivities).

> ...those are the best-constituted bodies, and have the longest existence, which possess the intrinsic means of frequently renewing themselves, or such as obtain this renovation in con sequence of some extrinsic accidents. And it is a truth clearer than light that, without such renovation, these bodies cannot continue to exist; and the means of renewing them is to bring them back to their original principles. For, as all religious republics and monarchies must have within themselves some goodness, by means of which they obtain their first growth and reputation, and as in the process of time this goodness becomes corrupted, it will of necessity destroy the body unless something intervenes to bring it back to its normal condition. Thus, the doctors of medicine say, in speaking of the human body, that "every day some ill humors gather which must be cured."[9]

Social Ethics

Proper conduct, especially for a ruler, is doing what is necessary to get and keep power. A society's power and stability are its highest values, for Machiavelli.

> And it must be understood that a prince, and especially a new prince, cannot observe all those things which are considered good in men, being often obliged, in order to maintain the state, to act against faith, against charity, against humanity, and against religion. And, therefore, he must have a mind disposed to adapt itself according to the wind, and as the variations of fortune dictate, and, as I said before, not deviate from what is good, if possible, but be able to do evil if constrained.[10]

Even religion should be employed to give order and stability to the state. Machiavelli believes that if religious faith has any value, it is in making the society powerful, obedient and loyal.

---

8   Machiavelli, pp. 237-238.
9   Machiavelli, pp. 397-398.
10 Machiavelli, p. 66.

Numa, finding a very savage people, and wishing to reduce them to civil obedience by the arts of peace, had recourse to religion as the most necessary and assured support of any civil society; and he established it upon such foundations that for many centuries there was nowhere more fear of the gods than in that republic, which greatly facilitated all the enterprises which the Senate [initiated]....And whoever reads Roman his tory attentively will see in how great a degree religion served in the command of the armies, in uniting the people and keeping them well conducted, and in covering the wicked with shame.[11]

For the same reason, it is useful for the Prince to *appear* religious even though he does not believe in or practice his religion.

It is not, therefore, necessary for a prince to have all the above-named qualities, but it is very necessary to seem to have them. I would even be bold to say that to possess them and always to observe them is dangerous, but to appear to possess them is useful. Thus it is well to seem merciful, faithful, humane, sincere, religious, and also to be so; but you must have the mind so disposed that when it is needful to be otherwise you may be able to change to the opposite....

A prince must take great care that nothing goes out of his mouth which is not full of the above-named five qualities, and, to see and hear him, he should seem to be all mercy, faith, integrity, humanity, and religion. And nothing is more necessary than to seem to have this last quality, for men in general judge more by the eyes than by the hands, for every one can see, but very few have to feel. Everybody sees what you appear to be, few feel what you are, and those few will not dare to oppose themselves to the many, who have the majesty of the state to defend them; and in the actions of men, and especially of princes, from which there is no appeal, the end justifies the means. Let a prince therefore aim at conquering and maintaining the state, and the means will always be judged honourable and praised by every one, for the vulgar is always taken by appearances....[12]

To do this, Machiavelli insists that the Prince must know how to develop the "beast" in himself, or rather two beasts: the lion and the fox; a successful Prince must be both fierce and shrewd.

A prince being thus obliged to know well how to act as a beast must imitate the fox and the lion, for the lion cannot protect himself from traps, and the fox cannot defend himself from wolves. One must therefore be a fox to recognise traps, and a lion to frighten wolves. Those that wish to be only lions do not understand this.

---

11 Machiavelli, pp. 146-147.
12 Machiavelli, pp. 65-66.

Therefore, a prudent ruler ought not to keep faith when by so doing it would be against his interest, and when the reasons which made him bind himself no longer exist. If men were all good, this precept would not be a good one; but as they are bad, and would not observe their faith with you, so you are not bound to keep faith with them.[13]

Machiavelli's manual of power politics, *The Prince*, concludes with an appeal to Lorenzo di Medici to use its "realism" to conquer all of Italy and restore the Roman Empire, elevating the Prince to Emperor.

---

13 Machiavelli, p. 64.

· 8 ·

THOMAS HOBBES

British Liberalism

Thomas Hobbes (1588-1679) is considered the father of British liberalism. The concepts of individual rights, liberty and contractual government originate in Hobbes' political theory. He was born in Malmesbury, England, and educated at Oxford. His life spanned the tumultuous period of the English Civil War, the experience of which, some attribute his fear of social upheaval and violence. Hobbes served as a tutor to the noble Devonshire family and, in that capacity, travelled throughout Europe. He conferred with the great scientific minds of the age and adapted modern scientific materialism to the study of politics. His major book, *Leviathan*, develops a "science of politics," whose methodology underlies much of twentieth-century Social Science, especially Behaviorism. Hobbes' emphasis on *power* as the end of all human activity, places him firmly in the Modern tradition, after Machiavelli.

Hobbesian political philosophy provides an extremely logical, internally-consistent view of human nature, political society and social ethics. The simplicity of his thought partially explains its appeal and endurance. Its atheism, materialism and advocacy of absolutist monarchy based on force and terror alienated Parliamentarians and Royalists alike. Hobbes' theories were considered so objectionable by the seventeenth-century English, that when the Great Fire of 1666 destroyed much of London, many blamed it on God's wrath over

Hobbes' writings. Parliament passed a law forbidding atheistic books, mentioning Hobbes by name, and thereafter he could not get his work published. Despite these early setbacks, Hobbes' ideas created quite a following and their premises and logic undergird much of Modern Western thought.

Human Nature

Hobbes explains human nature scientifically: man is understood in terms of "matter in motion." That which causes people to move is either Appetite (moving toward pleasure) or Aversion (moving away from pain).[1] All human activity is to be understood in purely physical terms. Man knows the world through material data striking his senses and he moves towards those sensations that please him and away from those sensations that hurt.

> Concerning the Thoughts of man, I will consider them first *Singly*, and afterwards in *Trayne*, or dependance upon one another. *Singly*, they are every one a *Representation* or *Apparence*, of some quality, or other Accident of a body without us; which is commonly called an *Object*. Which Object worketh on the Eyes, Eares, and other parts of mans body; and by diversity of working, produceth diversity of Apparences.
>
> The Originall of them all, is that which we call SENSE; (For there is no conception in a mans mind, which hath not at first, totally, or by parts, been begotten upon the organs of Sense.) The rest are derived from that originall....
>
> And this *seeming*, or *fancy*, is that which men call *Sense*; and consisteth, as to the Eye, in a *Light*, or *Colour figured*; To the Eare, in a *Sound*; To the Nostrill, in an *Odour*; To the Tongue and Palat, in a *Savour*; And to the rest of the body, in *Heat, Cold, Hardnesse, Softnesse*, and such other qualities as we discern by *Feeling*. All which qualities called *Sensible*, are in the object that causeth them, but so many severall motions of the matter,....[2]
>
> This Endeavour, when it is toward something which causes it, is called APPETITE, or DESIRE; the later, being the generall name; and the other, oftentimes restrayned to signifie the Desire of Food, namely *Hunger* and *Thirst*. And when the Endeavour is fromward something, it is generally called AVERSION. These words *Appetite,*

---

1   Thomas Hobbes, *Leviathan*, edited by C. B. Macpherson (Baltimore, Penguin, 1975), pp. 118-119.

2   Hobbes, pp. 85-86.

and *Aversion* we have from the *Latines*; and they both of them signifie the motions, one of approaching, the other of retiring.³

Therefore, all knowledge comes from appearance and all activity is motivated by physical desire. This materialism contrasts sharply with Classical Greek and Christian thought; Aristotle explained action in terms of collective reasoning and ethics, St. Thomas Aquinas in terms of reason informed by Divine and Natural Law. For Hobbes, reason is merely a calculating function, adding and subtracting sense data, cataloguing pleasures and pains. Dreams are not the voice of God or our subconscious, but "decaying" sense perception.⁴ Such radical empiricism shocked the philosophers and Churchmen of his time, but Hobbes' materialism has gained respectability in our own time through Behaviorist Social Science.

Hobbes' scientific view of human nature provided a developed explanation of Machiavelli's obsession with power. From Hobbes' materialist premises, power does become the beginning and end of all politics. In his chapter, "The Power, Worth and Dignity of Man," Hobbes shows that man's quest for pleasure invariably entangles him in a quest for power.

> The POWER *of a Man*, (to take it Universally), is his present means, to obtain some future apparent Good. And is either *Originall*, or *Instrumentall*.
>
> *Naturall Power*, is the eminence of the Faculties of Body, or Mind; as extraordinary Strength, Forme, Prudence, Arts, Eloquence, Liberality, Nobility. *Instrumentall* are those Powers, which acquired by these, or by fortune, are means and Instruments to acquire more: as Riches, Reputation, Friends, and the secret working of God, which men call Good Luck. For the nature of Power, is in this point, like to Fame, increasing as it proceeds; or like the motion of heavy bodies, which the further they go, make still the more hast.⁵

A person's power, therefore, can be divided into "Natural Power" (his strength of body and mind) and "Instrumental Power" (his money, reputation, connections, etc.) That power determines how well he will be able to satisfy his physical desires.

The "worth" of a person, therefore, is determined by the amount of power he possesses. Wealthy people are "worth" more for Hobbes, because they have

---

3   Hobbes, p. 119.
4   Hobbes, pp. 90-91.
5   Hobbes, p. 150.

more power to obtain the things they want. One laborer is "worth" more than another because he is stronger and can produce more work for his employer. So, a person's worth is determined, like any other product, by the market.

> The *Value*, or WORTH of a man, is as of all other things, his Price; that is to say, so much as would be given for the use of his Power; and therefore is not absolute; but a thing dependent on the need and judgement of another.[6]

Likewise, a person's "dignity" is measured by the amount of public honor, esteem and prestige he commands. Such esteem increases his power and ability to get what he wants.

> The publique worth of a man, which is the Value set on him by the Commonwealth, is that which men commonly call DIGNITY. And this Value of him by the Common-wealth, is understood, by offices of Command, Judicature, publike Employment; or by Names and Titles, introduced for distinction of such Value.[7]

Such definitions of human worth and dignity would confuse the Classical and Christian minds of Hobbes' time; for Aristotle would distinguish worth in moral excellence and St. Thomas Aquinas would distinguish it in God's creation and aspirations to the goodness of Divine Law. To both, Hobbes' materialism and hedonism would simply be the expressions of a vulgar, base mind, or the manifestation of Plato's appetitive spirit.

Hobbes' conception of human nature reduces all quality to power and all power to the satisfaction of individual desire. But such a conception produces a reality that frustrates human desire and establishes absolute power in the State.

Political Society

The vision of society that emerges from Hobbes' human nature is one of fierce competition amongst avaricious individuals. Each person pursuing his own desires causes inevitable conflict. Therefore, the original "society" of human beings (or the State of Nature) is a jungle existence, in which individuals of equal liberty take what they desire and destroy others. Hobbes calls this natural condition a war of "all against all," in which no security or peace can exist.

---

6   Hobbes, p. 151.
7   Hobbes, p. 151.

And because the condition of Man, (as hath been declared in the precedent Chapter) is a condition of Warre of every one against every one; in which case every one is governed by his own Reason; and there is nothing he can make use of, that may not be a help unto him, in preserving his life against his enemyes; It followeth, that in such a condition, every man has a Right to every thing; even to one anothers body. And there fore, as long as this naturall Right of every man to every thing endureth, there can be no security to any man....[8]

Such insecurity affects even the strong and wealthy, for as Hobbes is careful to point out, people are all *equal* in being able to murder each other (even if the weaker must conspire to do so against the stronger, or when he is sleeping).

Nature hath made men so equall, in the faculties of body, and mind; as that though there bee found one man sometimes manifestly stronger in body, or of quicker mind than another; yet when all is reckoned together, the difference between man, and man, is not so considerable, as that one man can thereupon claim to himselfe any benefit, to which another may not pre tend, as well as he. For as to the strength of body, the weakest has strength enough to kill the strongest, either by secret machination, or by confederacy with others, that are in the same danger with himselfe.[9]

Such a condition ruins man's chances for civilization and pleasure, and renders life "solitary, poore, nasty, brutish and short."

Whatsoever therefore is consequent to a time of Warre, where every man is Enemy to every man; the same is consequent to the time, wherein men live without other security, than what their own strength, and their own invention shall furnish them withall. In such condition, there is no place for Industry; because the fruit thereof is uncertain; and consequently no Culture of the Earth; no Navigation, nor use of the commodities that may be imported by Sea; no commodious Building; no instruments of moving, and removing such things as require much force; no Knowledge of the face of the Earth; no account of Time; no Arts; no Letters; no Society; and which is worst of all, continuall feare, and danger of violent death; And the life of man, solitary, poore, nasty, brutish and short.[10]

In this horrible condition of the State of Nature, man's Reason comes to the rescue. Reason, being for Hobbes that human faculty of calculation, tells man that it is not in his interest to have perfect liberty to take anything he wants

---

8   Hobbes, pp. 189–190.
9   Hobbes, p. 183.
10 Hobbes, p. 186.

if everyone else has equal liberty: he is outnumbered. So, Hobbes informs us that the First Law of Nature being Reason's forbidding man to do that which is destructive to his life, and the Second Law of Nature being that if liberty leads to the destructive State of Nature, then man's Reason leads him to give us his Natural Right to liberty and seek peace.

> ...consequently it is a precept, or generall rule of Reason, *That every man, ought to endeavour Peace, as farre as he has hope of obtaining it; and when he cannot obtain it, that he may seek, and use, all helps, and advantages of Warre.* The first branch of which Rule, containeth the first, and Fundamentall Law of Nature; which is, *to seek Peace, and follow it.* The Second, the summe of the Right of Nature; which is, *By all means we can, to defend our selves.*
>
> From this Fundamentall Law of Nature, by which men are commanded to endeavour Peace, is derived this second Law; *That a man be willing, when others are so too, as farre-forth, as for Peace, and defence of himselfe he shall think it necessary, to lay down this right to all things; and be contented with so much liberty against other men, as he would allow other men against himself.*[11]

This creates the basis for government. If every individual recognizes the dangers of absolute liberty in the State of Nature and agrees to surrender that liberty to a powerful Sovereign, they can enjoy peace. The State is formed through a "social contract" and given power to rule through the "consent of the governed." The people surrender their Natural Right to liberty to the Government which, in return, agrees to provide security from violent death, and peace.

> The finall Cause, End, or Designe of men, (who naturally love Liberty, and Dominion over others) in the introduction of that restraint upon themselves, (in which wee see them live in Common-wealths,) is the foresight of their own preservation, and of a more contented life thereby; that is to say, of getting themselves out from that miserable condition of Warre, which is necessarily consequent (as hath been shewn) to the naturall Passions of men when there is no visible Power to keep them in awe, and tye them by feare of punishment to the performance of their Covenants, and observation of those Lawes of Nature set down in the fourteenth and fifteenth Chapters.[12]
>
> The only way to erect such a Common power, as may be able to defend them from the invasion of Forraigners, and the injuries of one another, and thereby to secure them in such sort, as that by their owne industrie, and by the fruites of the Earth,

---

11 Hobbes, p. 190.
12 Hobbes, p. 223.

they may nourish themselves and live contentedly; is, to conferre all their power and strength upon one Man, or upon one Assembly of men, that may reduce all their Wills, by plurality of voices, unto one Will....to submit their Wills, every one to his Will, and their Judgements, to his Judgment. This is more than Consent, or Concord; it is a reall Unitie of them all, in one and the same Person, made by Covenant of every man with every man, in such manner, as if every man should say to every man, *I Authorise and give up my Right of Governing my selfe, to this Man, or to the Assembly of men, on this contition, that thou give up thy Right to him, and Authorise all his Actions in like manner.* This done, the Multitude so united in one Person, is called a COMMON-WEALTH, inlatine CIVITAS. This is the Generation of that great LEVIATHAN, or rather (to speake more reverently) of that *Mortall God*, to which wee owe under the *Immortall God*, our peace and defence.[13]

Given men's selfish propensities and tendency to break their promises when it suits them, the social contract must provide the "terror of some power" to "keep them in awe," and that is the State.[14] The people surrender their Natural Right to liberty and the State destroys anyone who does not abide by that surrendering. It thereby secures peace. To do so, the Sovereign must have control over all aspects of social life: regulation of property, censorship of the press, and rewarding of honors. Individuals retain only that basic right for which the State was created: life. They must be obedient to the Sovereign in all things until it comes to kill them; then they can resist.[15]

For Hobbes, the greatest threat to individual liberty is not a powerful State, but the anarchy of the State of Nature, i.e., the absence of a powerful State.

> ...the estate of Man can never be without some incommodity or other; and that the greatest, that in any forme of Government can possibly happen to the people, in generall, is scarce sensible, in respect of the miseries, and horrible calamities, that accompany a Civill Warre; or that dissolute condition of masterlesse men, without subjection to Lawes, and a coercive Power to tye their hands from rapine, and revenge....[16]

The need for a strong powerful government to punish violations of the peace becomes Hobbes' argument for monarchy: because a single ruler can more swiftly impose punishment on criminals. This is rather different from St. Thomas Aquinas' rationale for kingship.

---

13 Hobbes, p. 227.
14 Hobbes, pp. 223, 227.
15 Hobbes, pp. 233–237.
16 Hobbes, p. 238.

> ...the Resolutions of a Monarch, are subject to no other Inconstancy, than that of Humane Nature; but in Assemblies, besides that of Nature, there ariseth an Inconstancy from the Number. For the absence of a few, that would have the Resolution once taken, continue firme, (which may happen by security, negligence, or private impediments,) or the diligent appearance of a few of the contrary opinion, undoes to day, all that was concluded yesterday.[17]

But, regardless of the form of State, Hobbes wishes it to have absolute power, to crush the human tendency towards anarchy.

> So that it appeareth plainly, to my understanding, both from Reason, and Scripture, that the Soveraign Power, whether placed in One Man, as in Monarchy, or in one Assembly of men, as in Popular, and Aristocraticall Common-wealths, is as great, as possibly men can be imagined to make it. And though of so unlimited a Power, men may fancy many evill consequences, yet the consequences of the want of it, which is perpetuall warre of every man against his neighbour, are much worse. The condition of man in this life shall never be without Inconveniences; but there happeneth in no Common-wealth any great Inconvenience, but what proceeds from the Subjects disobedience, and breach of those Covenants, from which the Common-wealth hath its being. And whosoever thinking Soveraign Power too great, will seek to make it lesse; must subject himselfe, to the Power, that can limit it; that is to say, to a greater.[18]

Hobbes ridicules "democrats" who wish to limit the power of the State and compares their fear of Sovereign power to the fear of water characteristic of people afflicted with rabies.

> Which Venime I will not doubt to compare to the biting of a mad Dogge, which is a disease the Physicians call *Hydrophobia*, or *fear of Water*. For as he that is so bitten, has a continuall torment of thirst, and yet abhorreth water; and is in such an estate, as if the poyson endeavoured to convert him into a Dogge: So when a Monarchy is once bitten to the quick, by those Democraticall writers, that continually snarle at that estate; it wanteth nothing more than a strong Monarch, which nevertheless out of a certain *Tyrannophobia*, or feare of being strongly governed, when they have him, they abhorre.[19]

---

17 Hobbes, p. 242.
18 Hobbes, p. 260.
19 Hobbes, p. 370.

Social Ethics

The only social ethics that Hobbes' political theory prescribes is obedience to the State power. This will insure peace and whatever limited pleasure man can enjoy under such absolute rule. Otherwise, Hobbesian ethics are subjective and hedonistic. Because man's knowledge comes only from individual sense perception, any understanding of "the good" is private and personal. No objective standard of morality exists—only personal preference and opinion.

And, the basis for that personal determination of goodness is pleasure, or that which we like. Evil is that which does not feel good.

> But whatsoever is the object of any mans Appetite or Desire; that is it, which he for his part calleth *Good*: And the object of his Hate, and Aversion, *Evill*; And of his Contempt, *Vile*, and *Inconsiderable*. For these words of Good, Evill, and Contemptible, are ever used with relations to the person that useth them: There being nothing simply and absolutely so; nor any common Rule of Good and Evill, to be taken from the nature of the objects themselves; but from the Person of the man....*Pleasure* therefore, (or *Delight*,) is the apparence, or sense of Good; and *Molestation* or *Displeasure*, the apparence, or sense of Evill. And consequently all Appetite, Desire, and Love is accompanied with some Delight more or lesse; and all Hatred, and Aversion, with more or lesse Displeasure and Offence.[20]

Such identification of good and evil with individual, subjective preference begins "ethical relativism," with no standard of judgement above individual opinion (a position we are familiar with in modern American society). All "value judgements" are private and of equal value. One man's porridge is another man's poison. Who's to say. Abortion or private "lifestyles" are individual choices, with no one else capable of evaluating or passing judgement. This Hobbesian view contrasts with both Classical and Christian perspectives, which establish an objective standard of good and evil, either in the Golden Mean practiced by the excellent man or in the ideals of the City of God or Divine Law as known and taught by the Church. In *Leviathan*, Hobbes ridicules Aristotle as "Van Philosophy" and the Church's teachings as "the Kingdom of Fairies."[21]

Hobbesian ethics begin the Modern identification of pain and weakness with evil. The lack of power and wealth is the greatest of evils for Hobbes; pleasure is the greatest of goods. By implication, the poor and meek are also evil; they have no power, wealth or dignity and are a displeasure to those who do.

---

20 Hobbes, pp. 120, 122.
21 Hobbes, pp. 688, 712.

· 9 ·

JOHN LOCKE

Natural Rights

John Locke (1632–1704) is the most famous British liberal philosopher and the most influential on American political theory. Son of an officer in Cromwell's Puritan army, Locke inherited strong anti-monarchy sentiments. He was educated at Christ Church, Oxford, and participated in the Parliamentary struggles of the 1680's. His *Second Treatise of Government*, is considered a manifesto of limited, representative government that greatly affected the Parliamentary triumph in the Glorious Revolution of 1688.[1]

Human Nature

John Locke conceived of men in their natural state, or State of Nature, as "free, equal and independent."[2] The basis of this individual freedom, equality and independence (as in Hobbes) is man's material being: his physical senses and desires, and his power to follow and satisfy them.

---

1   See Peter Laslett's introduction to *Two Treatises of Government* by John Locke (New York, New American Library, 1965), pp. 58–72.
2   Locke, p. 374.

> To understand Political Power right, and derive it from its Original, we must consider what State all Men are naturally in, and that is, a State of Perfect Freedom to order their Actions, and dispose of their Possessions, and Persons as they think fit, within the bounds of the Law of Nature, without asking leave, or depending upon the Will of any other Man.
>
> A State also of Equality, wherein all the Power and Jurisdiction is reciprocal, no one having more than another: there being nothing more evident, than that Creatures of the same species and rank promiscuously born to all the same advantages of Nature, and the use of the same faculties, should also be equal one amongst another without Subordination or Subjection...[3]

This life of "perfect freedom" also includes the Natural Rights to Life, Liberty and Property, which are necessary to the continuation of that life (or "self preservation"). The only limit or restriction on individual freedom in the State of Nature is the "Law of Nature," known by Reason, which tells man that he can only enjoy his own liberty so long as he does not violate the liberty of others. In other words, for Locke, individuals in the State of Nature may freely enjoy their rights so long as they do not infringe upon the rights of others.

> But though this be a State of Liberty, yet it is not a State of Licence...The State of Nature has a Law of Nature to govern it, which obliges everyone: And Reason, which is that Law, teaches all Mankind, who will but consult it, that being all equal and independent, no one ought to harm another in his Life, Health, Liberty, or Possessions.[4]

Left to themselves, most men are reasonable, and will obey the Law of Nature, enjoying their own liberty without violating the rights of others to Life, Liberty and Property. And, if all men in the State of Nature were so self-controlled, there would never be any reason to establish government, for Locke. This is very different from Hobbes' view of man and society, where physical impulse would drive individuals to kill, enslave and rob others, only restrained by some overpowering State. For Locke, man's restraint is internal and reasonable men will limit their liberty to those actions which do not violate the rights of others.

The problem, for Locke, is that *some* people are *not* reasonable. Some men do not know, or disregard, the Law of Nature and willfully invade the rights of

---

3 Locke, p. 309.
4 Locke, p. 311.

others, stealing their property, enslaving their liberty or destroying their lives. Such persons are not fully human for Locke, because they do not use Reason.

> ...such Men are not under the ties of the Common Law of Reason, have no other Rule, but that of Force and Violence, and so may be treated as Beasts of Prey.[5]

That is, they may be killed, as a "Wolf or a Lyon,"[6] because in the State of Nature, every individual possesses the right to defend himself against transgressors of The Law of Nature.

> ...that all Men may be restrained from invading others Rights, and from doing hurt to one another, and the Law of Nature be observed...every one has a right to punish the transgressors of that Law....every Man hath a Right to punish the Offender, and be Executioner of the Law of Nature.[7]

The problem with this "private justice" in the State of Nature is that where individuals punish transgressors of their rights, they will serve as judges in their own cases and, Locke quickly points out, individuals cannot be fair and impartial judges in cases that directly affect themselves.

> ...it is unreasonable for Men to be Judges in their own Cases, that Self-Love will make Men partial to themselves and their Friends. And, on the other side, that Ill nature, Passion and Revenge will carry them too far in punishing others.[8]

Government is established, for Locke, to provide an impartial judge to determine violations of the Law of Nature and punish transgressors of others' rights to Life, Liberty and Property. "Civil Government is the proper Remedy for the Inconveniences of the State of Nature..."[9] Thus, Locke creates Government by consent of the governed out of a State of Nature where all individuals are "free, equal and independent."

But, because it is established by the majority of "law abiding" citizens to protect them against the few who violate others' rights, the Government is charged with protecting the Natural Rights of Life, Liberty and Property. Locke's State is, therefore, considerably more limited than Hobbes'. Locke's limited, consensual government is the equivalent of a policeman, or what we today call the

---

5 Locke, p. 319.
6 Locke, p. 319.
7 Locke, pp. 312-313.
8 Locke, p. 316.
9 Locke, p. 316.

"criminal justice system." It protects innocent people's rights to the peaceful enjoyment of life, liberty and property and punishes criminals who violate those Natural Rights. Otherwise, the State is supposed to leave you alone.

Political Society

Locke describes the emergence of government through a "Social Contract" from the inconveniences of the State of Nature, and its charge to protect individuals' Natural Rights to Life, Liberty and Property.

> Man being born, as has been proved, with a Title to perfect Freedom, and an uncontrouled enjoyment of all the Rights and Privileges of the Law of Nature, equally with any other Man, or Number of Men in the World, hath by Nature a Power, not only to preserve his Property, that is, his Life, Liberty and Estate, against the Injuries and Attempts of other men; but to judge of, and punish the breaches of that Law in others...But because no Political Society can be, nor subsist without having in itself the Power to preserve the Property, and in order thereunto punish the offences of all those of that Society; there, and there only is Political Society, where every one of the Members hath quitted this natural Power, resign'd it up into the hands of the Community ...the Community comes to be Umpire, by settling standing Rules, indifferent, and the same to all Parties; and by Men having Authority from the Community, for the execution of those Rules, decides all the differences that may happen before any Members of that Society...
>
> Those who are united into one Body, and have a common establish'd Law and Judicature to Appeal to, with Authority to decide Controversies between them, and punish Offenders, are in Civil Society one with another; but those who have no such common Appeal...are still in the state of Nature.[10]

A Lockean government, therefore, is one established by the consent of the governed to preserve property by applying laws equally and impartially (which is where Americans get the concept of "equality before the law" and "equal protection of the laws" in the 14th Amendment to the United States Constitution). The origin of this liberal government is the dangers and inconveniences of the State of Nature. Men are willing to give up their right to punish transgressors of the Law of Nature in exchange for a government that fairly arbitrates violations of Natural Rights, but otherwise leaves individuals alone to the "secure enjoyment of their properties."

---

10 Locke, p. 367.

> If Man in the State of Nature be so free, as has been said; If he be absolute Lord of his own Person and Possessions, equal to the greatest, and subject to no body, why will he part with his Freedom? Why will he give up this Empire, and subject himself to the Dominion and Controul of any other Power? To which 'tis obvious to Answer, that though in the state of Nature he hath such a right, yet the Enjoyment of it is very uncertain, and constantly exposed to the invasion of others. For all being Kings as much as he, every Man his Equal,... he has in this State [enjoyment] very unsafe, very insecure. This makes him willing to quit a Condition, which, however free, is full of fears and continual dangers; And 'tis not without reason that he seeks out, and is willing to joyn in Society with others...for the mutual Preservation of their Lives, Liberties and Estates, which I call by the general Name Property.[11]

Thus, for Locke, naturally free individuals establish Government to enhance their freedom and property rights.

> The great and chief end therefore, of Mens uniting into Commonwealths, and putting themselves under Government, is the Preservation of their Property.[12]

Since government is established to *preserve* Natural Rights, the State itself cannot invade the individual's rights to Life, Liberty and Property, but is charged to protect those rights (unlike Hobbes' absolutist State, or later, Marx's socialist State).

> But though Men when they enter into Society, give up the Equality, Liberty and Executive Power they had in the State of Nature...yet it being only with an intention in every one the better to preserve himself his Liberty and Property[13]... a Man... cannot, by Compact, or his own Consent, enslave himself under the Absolute, Arbitrary Power of another...[14]

If a State becomes an "Absolute, Arbitrary Power," or what Locke would simply call a "Tyranny," which, rather than protecting individual rights to Life, Liberty and Property, invades those rights itself, the people have a right to overthrow that government. This "Right to Revolution" against unjust government went straight from Locke's Second Treatise into Thomas Jefferson's Declaration

---

11 Locke, p. 395.
12 Locke, p. 395.
13 Locke, p. 398.
14 Locke, p. 325.

of Independence.[15] In both, a Tyranny was charged with usurping the legitimate function of government (preserving individual rights) and establishing a State of War against the citizenry.

> As Usurpation is the exercise of Power, which another hath a Right to; so Tyranny is the exercise of Power beyond Right, which no Body can have a right to. And this is making use of the Power any one has in his hands; not for the good of those who are under it, but for his own private separate Advantage...his Commands and Actions are not directed to the preservation of the Properties of his People, but the satisfaction of his own Ambition, Revenge, Covetousness, or any other irregular Passion.[16]

Such tyranny "dissolves" the Social Contract and the people's allegiance to the government. The people are now free to establish a new government which will properly preserve the rights of Nature.

> The Reason why Men enter into Society is the preservation of their Property... whenever the Legislators endeavor to take away, and destroy the Property of the People, or to reduce them to Slavery under Arbitrary Power, they put themselves into a state of War with the People, who are thereupon absolved from any further Obedience...[17]

> ...such Revolutions happen not upon every little mismanagement in publick affairs. Great mistakes in the ruling part, many wrong and inconvenient Laws, and all the slips of human frailty will be born by the people, without mutiny or murmur. But if a long train of Abuses, Prevarications, and Artifices, all tending the same way, make the design visible to the People, and they cannot but feel, what they lie under, and see, whither they are going, 'tis not to be wonder'd, that they should then rouze themselves, and endeavor to put the rule into such hands, which may secure to them the ends for which Government was at first erected...[18]

Thomas Jefferson's Declaration of Independence draws not merely on Locke's revolutionary justification, but also on the Lockean theory of human nature and consentual government:

---

15 See my article, "John Locke in Jefferson's Declaration of Independence," *Virginia Social Science Journal*, Winter, 1984.
16 Locke, p. 446.
17 Locke, p. 460.
18 Locke, pp. 463–464.

We hold these truths to be sacred & undeniable; that all men are created equal & independent, that from that equal creation they derive rights inherent and inalienable, among which are the preservation of life, & liberty, & the pursuit of happiness; and to secure these ends, governments are instituted among men, deriving their just powers from the consent of the governed; that whenever any form of government shall become destructive of these ends, it is the right of the people to alter or to abolish it & to institute new government,...prudence indeed will dictate that governments long established should not be changed for light & transient causes: and accordingly all experience hath shewn that mankind are more disposed to suffer while evils are sufferable than to right themselves...but when a long train of abuses & usurpations, begun at a distinguished period, & pursued invariably the same object, evinces a design to subject them to arbitrary power, it is their right, it is their duty, to throw off such government & to provide new guards for their future security.[19]

So, American independence from Great Britain was justified on Lockean terms, and the subsequent U. S. Constitution is often regarded as our "Social Contract," to secure the Natural Rights of Life, Liberty and Property.[20]

Property

Since Locke's concept of property is central to his understanding of both Human Nature and Political Society (property comes from human labour and sustains life, and government is created to preserve property), it seems fitting to examine more closely his concept of property.

> And 'tis not without reason, that he seeks out, and is willing to joyn in Society with others, who are already united, or have a mind to unite for the mutual preservation of their Lives, Liberties and Estates, which I call by the general Name Property.

> The great and chief end therefore, of Mens uniting into Commonwealths, and putting themselves under Government, is the Preservation of their Property.[21]

---

19   *The Papers of Thomas Jefferson*, Volume I, edited by Julian Boyd (Princeton, Princeton University Press, 1950), pp. 423-424.

20   For specific references to life, liberty and property in the United States Constitution, see Amendments Five and Fourteen.

21   Locke, p. 395.

This emphasis on private property has caused some to accuse Locke of being an apologist for emerging capitalism in England.[22] While this interpretation may be overdrawn, Locke's formulation of the origins and prerogatives of private property certainly reveals the complementarity of political liberalism with free market capitalism.

Locke begins by asserting the traditional Christian (Thomist) view of property: that God gave the earth to mankind in common.

> Whether we consider natural Reason, which tells us that Men, being once born, have a right to their Preservation, and consequently to Meet and Drink and such other things as Nature affords for their Subsistence: Or Revelation which gives us an account of those Grants God made of the World to Adam and Noah, and his Sons, 'tis very clear that God, as King David says, Psal. CXV. xvi has given the Earth to the Children of Men, given it to mankind in common.[23]

He quickly, however, shows how that common Divine bequest was divided into private property, to the benefit of man. God, Locke explains, gave the earth to man to be used to his greatest advantage, which requires some means for individuals to appropriate the fruits of the earth as they need them.

> God, who hath given the World to Men in Common, hath also given them reason to make use of it to the best advantage of Life and convenience. The Earth, and all that is therein, is given to Men for the support and comfort of their being. And though all the fruits it naturally produces, and the Beasts it feeds, belong to Mankind in common...there must of necessity be a means to appropriate them some way or other before they can be of any use or at all beneficial to any particular Man.[24]

That means of appropriation is man's *labour*—the physical strength of his body which is his first "possession." The mixing of one's labour with the common fruits of the earth, for Locke, produces legitimate title to private property.

> The Labour of his Body, and the work of his Hands, we may say, are properly his. Whatsoever, then he removes out of the State that Nature hath provided, and left it in, he hath mixed his Labour with, and joyned to it something that is his own, and thereby makes it his Property.[25]

---

22 C. B. Macpherson, *The Political Theory of Possessive Individualism* (Oxford, 1962).
23 Locke, p. 327.
24 Locke, p. 328.
25 Locke, p. 329.

This "labour theory of value" (later taken up by Marx), argues that all new value comes from man's mixing his labour with nature, and that this also creates legitimate title to private property ownership.

> 'tis Labour indeed that puts the difference of value on every thing...'Tis Labour then which puts the greatest part of Value upon Land, without which it would scarcey be worthy any thing: 'tis to that we owe the greatest part of all its useful Products: for all that the Straw, Bran, Bread, of that acre of Wheat, is more worth than the Product of an acre of as good Land, which lies waste, is all the Effect of Labour. For 'tis not barely the Ploughman's Pains, the Reaper's and Thresher's Toil, and the Baker's Sweat, is to be counted into the Bread we eat, the Labour of those who broke the Oxen, who digged and wrought the Iron and Stones, who felled and framed the Timber imployed about the Plough, Mill, Oven, or any other Utensils, which are a vast Number, requisite to this Corn, from its being seed to be sown to its being made Bread, must all be charged on the account of Labour.[26]

And, while labour created value in property, for Locke, it also "gave a Right of property,"[27] which meant that that which I produced with my labour became *mine*.

However, Locke insists (again, after the manner of St. Thomas Aquinas) that there is a "natural" limit to the amount of property one can accumulate, even through one's labour. That limit is how much one can *use* before it spoils, as God did not give us wealth to be wasted.

> The same Law of Nature that does by this means give us Property, does also bound that property too. God has given us all things richly, 1 Tim. vi 17. is the voice of Reason confirmed by Inspiration. But how far has he given it us? To enjoy. As much as any one can make use of to any advantage of life before it spoils: so much he may be his labour fix a Property in. Whatever is beyond this, is more than this share, and belongs to others. Nothing was made by God for Man to spoil or destroy.[28]

This "spoilage" limitation to the accumulation of property greatly restricts wealth until the invention of money in gold and silver-metals that do not decay. Currency, for Locke, removes the natural limits on the accumulation of wealth by overcoming the spoilage standard.

---

26 Locke, p. 340.
27 Locke, p. 341.
28 Locke, p. 332.

> That the same Rule of Property (viz.) that every Man should have as much as he could make use of, would hold still in the World, without straitning any body, since there is Land enough in the World to suffice double the Inhabitants had not the Invention of Money and the tacit agreement of Men to put value on it, introduced (by Consent) larger Possessions, and a Right to them;...[Men] had agreed that a little piece of yellow Metal, which would keep without wasting or decay, should be worth a great piece of Flesh, or a whole heap of Corn...[29]

This invention of money also allowed another aspect of capitalism: wage labor. In his description of the Labour Theory of Value, Locke makes this interesting statement:

> Thus the Grass my Horse has bit;
> the Turfs my Servant has cut;
> and the Ore I have digg'd
> in any place where I have
> a right to them in common
> with others, become my Property...[30]

The question immediately arises (especially for Karl Marx, 200 years later), why does "my Servant's" labour become my property rather than his own? Locke's answer gives one of the earliest statements of capitalist wage labour. Apparently, at some point in society, all the nature held in common is appropriated,[31] or perhaps some men prefer to work for others rather than strike out on their own. In any event, the wage-labourer, or "servant," owns property in his body (and its labour) which he can sell to someone who possesses accumulated value (in gold). This arrangement is a "free contract" for Locke, because each enters it voluntarily and the employer's power over the servant only extends over the period of employment.

> ...a Freeman makes himself a Servant to another, by selling him for a certain time, the Service he undertakes to do, in exchange for Wages he is to receive. And though this commonly puts him into the Family of his Master, and under the ordinary Discipline thereof; yet it gives the Master but a Temporary Power over him, and no greater, than what is contained in the Contract between 'em.[32]

---

29 Locke, pp. 335-366.
30 Locke, p. 330.
31 Locke, p. 341.
32 Locke, pp. 365-366.

As we shall see, Rousseau, Marx and others question the "freedom" of the wagelabour contract, and the effects on politics of extremes of wealth and poverty. But, Locke's argument comes directly to contemporary American politics through the conservative ideology of Ronald Reagan, and its call for reduced government spending, limited government and increased free enterprise.

For Locke, labour is "property" as much as capital (accumulated wealth), and the government is established to preserve property. The government protects the Natural Rights to Life, Liberty and Estate by securing the wealthy from thieves and protecting the poor's right to sell their labour. If it thus treats everyone "equally" in this sense, it is serving the legitimate function of government and it should not be subject to revolution. And all, rich or poor, who benefit from the security and services it provides (even those "bearly travelling freely on the Highway"),[33] are obliged to obey the government and its laws.

Thus, Locke's political theory is radical in its individualism and its emphasis on freedom, equality and independence, but it is conservative in protecting the results of that individualism.

Social Ethics

John Locke's social ethics may be termed "negative" in that their standard of goodness is what one does not do to others. Basically, one is an ethical person in society if one does *not* violate the Natural Rights of others. Locke describes this ethic through his concept of The Law of Nature. According to this Law, known by Reason, each individual is free to "order their Actions and dispose of their Possessions, and Persons as they think fit...without asking leave, or depending on the Will of any other Man."[34] This freedom to do as one pleases is only limited by the similar rights of others. So, each individual for Locke has rights to Life, Liberty and Property so long as their actions do not disturb others' rights to Life, Liberty and Property.

> The State of Nature has a Law of Nature to govern it, which obliges everyone: And Reason, which is that Law, teaches all Mankind, who will but consult it, that being all equal and independent, no one ought to harm another in his Life, Health, Liberty, or Possession.[35]

---

33 Locke, p. 392.
34 Locke, p. 309.
35 Locke, p. 311.

Therefore, to be "good" to another person one must (1) not violate their rights to Life, Liberty and Property (i.e., do not injure, enslave or steal from them) and (2) leave them free to enjoy their liberty and property as they see fit (i.e., "mind your own business"). This social ethic is quite familiar to Americans and it conforms nicely with laissez-faire capitalism. But, it assumes a certain independence of individuals, and their actions, which has lately been called into question. In an increasingly complex and interdependent world, this Lockean claim of individual independence and autonomy may seem anachronistic. However, negative Lockean ethics remain strong in American society: from the Pro-Choice advocates in the Abortion controversy to Robert Nozick's recent book criticizing the Welfare State (see Chapter 19). America, with its vast expanse and material wealth is probably the most Lockean society on earth, where individuals can still claim the right to freedom in thought, expression, action, and property; but even here, it is becoming increasingly evident that private actions of many kinds have inevitable public consequences.

· 10 ·

JEAN JACQUES ROUSSEAU

French Liberalism

Jean Jacques Rousseau (1712-1778) is the leading French liberal political theorist. He was born in Geneva, Switzerland; his mother died giving birth to him. Rousseau's father was a watchmaker and Jean Jacques received little formal education. At the age of 16, he ran away from home, wandering around France for several years and finally settling in Paris. In 1749, Rousseau won First Prize in an essay contest sponsored by The Academy of Dijon on whether the arts and sciences have corrupted or improved society. Rousseau's thesis, that man is by nature good, but corrupted by society, earned him instant notoriety. He subsequently wrote a *Second Discourse* on the origins of inequality and his most famous work in political theory, *The Social Contract*.

Rousseau is remembered as a highly eccentric and eclectic individual. Before going mad late in life, he contributed to a wide range of fields, including literature, drama, education and music. He enjoyed the society (despite frequent quarrels) of the Paris intellectuals who contributed to Diderot's *Encyclopedia*, and became acquainted with philosophers across Europe and Britain. Rousseau's emphasis on community and the General Will modifies the strongly individualistic strain of British liberalism. This has caused him to be praised by contemporary "communitarian" thinkers (such as Benjamin Barber) and denounced by traditional liberal scholars, who at times attribute "totalitarian" ideas to Rousseau's political theory.

Human Nature

Rousseau identified human nature, or man's condition in the State of Nature, with two qualities: a desire for self-preservation (or self-interest) and a capacity for sympathy (or other-interest). This places man's distinctive nature in his feelings or passions, which for Rousseau affects the rest of his development in political society.

> Throwing aside, therefore, all those scientific books, which teach us only to see men such as they have made themselves, and contemplating the first and most simple operations of the human soul, I think I can perceive in it two principles prior to reason, one of them deeply interesting us in our own welfare and preservation, and the other exciting a natural repugnance at seeing any other sensible being, and particularly any of our own species, suffer pain or death. It is from the agreement and combination which the understanding is in a position to establish between these two principles, without its being necessary to introduce that of sociability, that all the rules of natural right appear to me to be derived-rules which our reason is afterwards obliged to establish on other foundations, when by its successive developments it has been led to suppress nature itself.
>
> In proceeding thus, we shall not be obliged to make man a philosopher before he is a man. His duties toward others are not dictated to him only by the later lessons of wisdom; and, so long as he does not resist the internal impulse of compassion, he will never hurt any other man, nor even any sentient being, except on those lawful occasions on which his own preservation is concerned and he is obliged to give himself the preference.[1]

These two qualities reside in natural man, but are quickly corrupted by the vanity of civil society, which exaggerates a person's self-interest at the expense of his natural sympathy. This view that society corrupts man's natural goodness leads to Rousseau's reputation for elevating the "noble savage" over civilized man. Actually, Rousseau describes natural man as being in a state of innocence, not unlike Christians' Garden of Eden, in which he is neither good nor evil, possessing neither virtue nor vices.

---

1 Jean Jacques Rousseau, *A Discourse on the Origin of Inequality* in *The Social Contract and Discourses*, translated by G.D.H. Cole (New York, Dent Dutton, 1973), pp. 41-42.

> In instinct alone, he had all he required for living in the state of nature; and with a developed understanding he has only just enough to support life in society.
>
> It appears, at first view, that men in a state of nature, having no moral relations or determinate obligations one with another, could not be either good or bad, virtuous or vicious; unless we take these terms in a physical sense, and call, in an individual, those qualities vices which may be injurious to his preservation, and those virtues which contribute to it; in which case, he would have to be accounted most virtuous, who put least check on the pure impulses of nature....
>
> Above all, let us not conclude, with Hobbes, that because man has no idea of goodness, he must be naturally wicked; that he is vicious because he does not know virtue; that he always refuses to do his fellow-creatures services which he does not think they have a right to demand; or that by virtue of the right he justly claims to all he needs, he foolishly imagines himself the sole proprietor of the whole universe.[2]

Rousseau describes how this original innocence becomes first corrupted by society and then redeemed by politics. Originally, man lived in the wild with the beasts, relying on his natural strength and cunning.

> The body of a savage man being the only instrument he understands, he uses it for various purposes, of which ours, for want of practice, are incapable: for our industry deprives us of that force and agility which necessity obliges him to acquire. If he had had an axe, would he have been able with his naked arm to break so large a branch from a tree? If he had had a sling, would he have been able to throw a stone with so great velocity? If he had had a ladder, would he have been so nimble in climbing a tree? If he had had a horse, would he have been himself so swift of foot? Give civilized man time to gather all his machines about him, and he will no doubt easily beat the savage; but if you would see a still more unequal contest, set them together naked and unarmed, and you will soon see the advantage of having all our forces constantly at our disposal, of being always prepared for every event, and of carrying one's self, as it were, perpetually whole and entire about one.[3]

But, gradually, man developed technology and families grew into tribes and villages. This emergence of "society" corrupted man's innocent virtue. This occurred as strangers gathered for festivals and markets and individuals began comparing themselves with other individuals and both began being judged by the others around them. The vanity and insecurity that this competition

---

2   Rousseau, pp. 64–65.
3   Rousseau, p. 48.

produced increased everyone's desire for self-preservation and reduced their natural sympathy for others.

> They accustomed themselves to assemble before their huts round a large tree; singing and dancing, the true offspring of love and leisure, became the amusement, or rather the occupation, of men and women thus assembled together with nothing else to do. Each one began to consider the rest, and to wish to be considered in turn; and thus a value came to be attached to public esteem. Whoever sang or danced best, whoever was the handsomest, the strongest, the most dexterous, or the most eloquent, came to be of most consideration; and this was the first step towards inequality, and at the same time towards vice. From these first distinctions arose on the one side vanity and contempt and on the other shame and envy: and the fermentation caused by these new leavens ended by producing combinations fatal to innocence and happiness.
>
> As soon as men began to value one another, and the idea of consideration had got a footing in the mind, every one put in his claim to it, and it became impossible to refuse it to any with impunity. Hence arose the first obligations of civility even among savages; and every intended injury became an affront; because, besides the hurt which might result from it, the party injured was certain to find in it a contempt for his person, which was often more insupportable than the hurt itself.
>
> Thus, as every man punished the contempt shown him by others, in proportion to his opinion of himself, revenge became terrible, and men bloody and cruel.[4]

Such insecure vanity and ruthless competition was eventually extended, for Rousseau, into property and law–which served to further protect the individual's fragile ego.

> The cultivation of the earth necessarily brought about its distribution; and property, once recognized, gave rise to the first rules of justice; for, to secure each man his own, it had to be possible for each to have something. Besides, as men began to look forward to the future, and all had something to lose, every one had reason to apprehend that reprisals would follow any injury he might do to another....
>
> It now became the interest of men to appear what they really were not. To be and to seem became two totally different things; and from this distinction sprang insolent pomp and cheating trickery, with all the numerous vices that go in their train. On the other hand, free and independent as men were before, they were not, in consequence of a multiplicity of new wants, brought into subjection, as it were, to

---

4 Rousseau, pp. 81–82.

all nature, and particularly to one another; and each became in some degree a slave even in becoming the master of other men: if rich, they stood in need of the services of others; if poor, of their assistance; and even a middle condition did not enable them to do without one another. Man must now, therefore, have been perpetually employed in getting others to interest themselves in his lot, and in making them, apparently at least, if not really, find their advantage in promoting his own. Thus he must have been sly and artful in his behavior to some, and imperious and cruel to others; being under a kind of necessity to ill-use all the persons of whom he stood in need, when he could not frighten them into compliance, and did not judge it his interest to be useful to them. Insatiable ambition, the thirst of raising their respective fortunes, not so much from real want as from the desire to surpass others, inspired all men with a vile propensity to injure one another, and with a secret jealousy, which is the more dangerous, as it puts on the mask of benevolence, to carry its point with greater security. In a word, there arose rivalry and competition on the one hand, and conflicting interests on the other, together with a secret desire on both of profiting at the expense of others. All these evils were the first effects of property, and the inseparable attendants of growing inequality.[5]

Rousseau's description of social life as a kind of theater, in which individuals are on stage and judged by critics, conforms to his writings on drama and the corrupting effect of theater on actors and actresses.[6] Both subject the individual to an "audience" and compare his appearance to that of others. This causes every one to become vain and more concerned with appearance than substance. As Rousseau describes the civilized life of Paris:

> Civilized peoples, cultivate such pursuits; to them, happy slaves, you owe that delicacy and exquisiteness of taste, which is so much your boast, that sweetness of disposition and urbanity of manners which make intercourse so easy and agreeable among you—in a word, the appearance of all the virtues, without being in possession of one of them.

It was this sort of refined civilization, all the more attractive for its apparent lack of ostentation, which distinguished Athens and Rome in those most celebrated days of their splendour and magnificence: and it is doubtless in the same respect that our own age and nation will excel all periods and peoples. An air of philosophy without pedantry; an address at once natural and engaging, distant equally from Teutonic rusticity and Italian pantomime; these are the effects of a taste acquired by liberal studies and improved by conversation with the world. What happiness

---

5   Rousseau, pp. 85-87.
6   Jean Jacques Rousseau, *Letter to M. D'Alembert on the Theatre* in *Politics and the Arts*, translated by Allan Bloom (Ithaca, 1977).

> would it be for those who live among us, if our external appearance were always a true mirror of our hearts; if decorum were but virtue; if the maxims we professed were the rules of our conduct; and if real philosophy were inseparable from the title of a philosopher! But so many good qualities too seldom go together; virtue rarely appears in so much pomp and state. Richness of apparel may proclaim the man of fortune, and elegance the man of taste; but true health and manliness are known by different signs. It is under the homespun of the labourer, and not beneath the gilt and tinsel of the courtier, that we should look for strength and vigour of body.[7]

Thus, the source of human evil is not man's nature, but "society." The remedy for this evil is not a return to savage simplicity, but a move forward to political society.

Political Society

The innocent virtue lost in civilized society is regained and refined, for Rousseau, in a certain kind of political society. The undeveloped, natural sympathy of the savage is cultivated in participatory democratic communities.

> The passage from the state of nature to the civil stage produces a very remarkable change in man, by substituting justice for instinct in his conduct, and giving his actions the morality they had formerly lacked. Then only, when the voice of duty takes the place of physical impulses and right of appetite, does man, who so far had considered only himself, find that he is forced to act on different principles, and to consult his reason before listening to his inclinations. Although in this state, he deprives himself of some advantages which he got from nature, he gains in return others so great, his faculties are so stimulated and developed, his ideas so extended, his feelings so ennobled, and his whole soul so uplifted, that, did not the abuses of this new condition often degrade him below that which he left, he would be bound to bless continually the happy moment which took him from it for ever, and, instead of a stupid and unimaginative animal, made him an intelligent being and a man.[8]

For Rousseau, the political community does this by addressing the perennial problem of political theory: how do individuals retain freedom while society gains order and justice?

---

7   Rousseau, *A Discourse on The Arts and Sciences* in Cole, p. 5.
8   Rousseau, *The Social Contract* in Cole, pp. 177-178.

'The problem is to find a form of association which will defend and protect with the whole common force the person and goods of each associate, and in which each, while uniting himself with all, may still obey himself alone, and remain as free as before.' This is the fundamental problem of which the social contract provides the solution.[9]

Rousseau's solution is through citizens' direct participation in the lawmaking of the community, each person then living under the rules he himself has made.

> We might, over and above all this, add, to what man acquires in the civil state, moral liberty, which alone makes him truly master of himself; for the mere impulse of appetite is slavery, while obedience to a law which we prescribe to ourselves is liberty.[10]

Rather than giving up his individual rights to another person (as in Hobbes) the participatory citizen gives up his individual rights to the whole community-of which he is a part, and therefore retains them.

> ...the total alienation of each associate, together with all his rights, to the whole community; for, in the first place, as each gives himself absolutely, the conditions are the same for all; and, this being so, no one has any interest in making them burdensome to others.
>
> Moreover, the alienation being without reserve, the union is as perfect as it can be, and no associate has anything more to demand; for, if the individuals retained certain rights, as there would be no common superior to decide between them and the public, each, being on one point his own judge, would ask to be so on all; the state of nature would thus continue, and the association would necessarily become inoperative or tyrannical.
>
> Finally, each man, in giving himself to all, gives himself to nobody; and as there is no associate over which he does not acquire the same right as he yields others over himself, he gains an equivalent for everything he loses, and an increase of force for the preservation of what he has.[11]

---

9   Rousseau, *The Social Contract* in Cole, p. 174.
10 Rousseau, *The Social Contract* in Cole, p. 174.
11 Rousseau, *The Social Contract* in Cole, p. 175.

Such giving over of the self to the whole community through the collective deliberation of lawmaking also produces the "General Will," or the expression of the public portion of the individual's nature.

> 'Each of us puts his person and all his power in common under the supreme direction of the general will, and, in our corporate capacity, we receive each member as an indivisible part of the whole.'
>
> At once, in place of the individual personality of each contracting party, this act of association creates a corporate and collective body, composed of as many members as the assembly contains voters, and receiving from this act its unity, its common identity, its life, and its will. This public person, so formed by the union of all other persons, formerly took the name of *city*, and now takes that of *Republic* or *body politic*; it is called by its members *State* when passive, *Sovereign* when active, and *Power* when compared with others like itself. Those who are associated in it take collectively the name of *people*, and severally are called *citizens*, as sharing in the sovereign authority, and *subjects*, as being under the laws of the State.[12]

Thus Rousseau, after Aristotle and St. Thomas Aquinas, sees the individual as part of a whole—a collective body of rational citizens whose "community interest" is identical with his "public" self. So, unlike the British liberals Hobbes and Locke, who conceive of man as naturally solitary and government as solely protecting individual rights, Rousseau sees man's natural capacity for sympathy as an inherently *social* or public instinct, which can be cultivated through rational participation in lawmaking. Law should reflect the common good, which the General Will defines, and this, for Rousseau, is the only legitimate basis for sovereignty.

> The first and most important deduction from the principles we have so far laid down is that the general will alone can direct the State according to the object for which it was instituted, i.e., the common good: for if the clashing of particular interests made the establishment of societies necessary, the agreement of these very interests made it possible. The common element in these different interests is what forms the social tie; and, were there no point of agreement between them all, no society could exist. It is solely on the basis of this common interest that every society should be governed.
>
> I hold then that Sovereignty, being nothing less than the exercise of the general will, can never be alienated, and that the Sovereign, who is no less than a collective

---

12 Rousseau, *The Social Contract* in Cole, p. 175.

being, cannot be represented except by himself: the power indeed may be transmitted, but not the will.[13]

British liberalism (and American pluralism), which sees no common good beyond private interest, for Rousseau cannot produce true law. This is partly because both rely on *representative* democracy, which alienates the General Will from the people.

> Sovereignty, for the same reason as makes it inalienable, is indivisible; for will either is, or is not, general; it is the will either of the body of the people, or only of a part of it. In the first case, the will, when declared, is an act of Sovereignty and constitutes law: in the second, it is merely a particular will, or act of magistracy—at the most a decree.[14]

The General Will, for Rousseau, is both *process* and a *product*. The process of the General Will requires an assembly of all citizens (like the Greek polis) and the free and full expression of all particular wills, after which, from public deliberation, the General Will or common good will emerge.

> There is often a great deal of difference between the will of all and the general will; the latter considers only the common interest, while the former takes private interest into account, and is no more than a sum of particular wills: but take away from these same wills the pluses and minuses that cancel one another, and the general will remains as the sum of the differences.[15]

As such, Rousseau has a notion of the public nature of human beings and the education of politics. Politics reconciles the reason and passion of individuals and the particular and general wills of society. An example of this might be a debate on public health policy. In American pluralism, all interest groups would lobby the government with the strongest reaping the most benefits. In Rousseau's state, all concerned would likewise express their particular wills (citizens for good care and reasonable costs, doctors for good salaries and equipment, taxpayers for reasonable tax rates, insurance companies for predictable increases, etc.). Out of all these particular expressions and the debate and discussion that follows, a consensus over a policy will emerge and this will be the General Will. Rather than the most powerful group prevailing or a "compromise" giving each

---

13 Rousseau, *The Social Contract* in Cole, p. 182.
14 Rousseau, *The Social Contract* in Cole, p. 183.
15 Rousseau, *The Social Contract* in Cole, p. 185.

group some benefit (commensurate with their influence), Rousseau foresees an entirely new policy that all agree on and that serves the common good.

The conditions necessary for such a *transforming* politics are a certain quality of citizenry, a certain standard of wealth and a certain kind of religion.

The first condition for Rousseau's polity is a cultured, educated, reasonable citizenry that is capable of democratic self-rule. Rousseau criticizes Peter the Great for ignoring this cultural capacity when he attempted to bring the Russian people into Enlightenment Europe.

> One people is amenable to discipline from the beginning; another, not after ten centuries. Russia will never be really civilized, because it was civilized too soon. Peter had a genius for imitation; but he lacked true genius, which is creative and makes all from nothing. He did some good things, but most of what he did was out of place. He saw that his people was barbarous, but did not see that it was not ripe for civilization; he wanted to civilize it when it needed only hardening. His first wish was to make Germans or Englishmen, when he ought to have been making Russians....[16]

Second, the state cannot be too large or populous, so that all citizens may participate in common deliberation.

> As nature has set bounds to the stature of a well-made man, and, outside those limits, makes nothing but giants or dwarfs, similarly, for the constitution of a State to be at its best, it is possible to fix limits that will make it neither too large for good government, nor too small for self-maintenance. In every body politic there is a maximum strength which it cannot exceed and which it only loses by increasing in size. Every extension of the social tie means its relaxation; and, generally speaking, a small State is stronger in proportion than a great one.[17]

Also, the republic must be of moderate wealth-relatively prosperous without extremes of wealth or poverty.

> I have already defined civil liberty; by equality, we should understand, not that the degrees of power and riches are to be absolutely identical for everybody; but that power shall never be great enough for violence, and shall always be exercised by virtue of rank and law; and that, in respect of riches, no citizen shall ever be wealthy enough to buy another, and none poor enough to be forced to sell himself; which

---

16 Rousseau, *The Social Contract* in Cole, p. 198.
17 Rousseau, *The Social Contract* in Cole, p. 199.

implies, on the part of the great, moderation in goods and postion, and, on the side of the common sort, moderation in avarice and covetousness....

> If the object is to give the State consistency, bring the two extremes as near to each other as possible; allow neither rich men nor beggars. These two estates, which are naturally inseparable, are equally fatal to the common good; from the one come the friends of tyranny, and from the other tyrants. It is always between them that public liberty is put up to auction; the one buys, and the other sells.[18]

Finally, Rousseau sees the need for a religion that reinforces the General Will: a "civil religion" that teaches social virtues and obviously neglects the elaborate rituals and offices of the Roman Catholic Church (and its identification, in France, with the Monarchy).

> Now, it matters very much to the community that each citizen should have a religion. That will make him love his duty; but the dogmas of that religion concern the State and its members only so far as they have reference to morality and to the duties which he who professes them is bound to do to others. Each man may have, over and above, what opinions he pleases, without its being the Sovereign's business to take cognizance of them; for, as the Sovereign has no authority in the other world, whatever the lot of its subjects may be in the life to come, that is not its business, provided they are good citizens in this life....
>
> The dogmas of civil religion ought to be few, simple, and exactly worded, without explanation or commentary. The existence of a mighty, intelligent, and beneficent Divinity, possessed of foresight and providence, the life to come, the happiness of the just, the punishment of the wicked, the sanctity of the social contract and the laws: these are its positive dogmas. Its negative dogmas I confine to one, intolerance, which is a part of the cults we have rejected.[19]

Rousseau's political theory influenced American thought primarily through the notion of "the Sovereign People." Otherwise, except for the occasional "communitarian" theorist (such as Benjamin Barber), it has been far less influential than Lockean liberalism.

---

18 Rousseau, *The Social Contract* in Cole, p. 204.
19 Rousseau, *The Social Contract* in Cole, pp. 275-276.

Social Ethics

Rousseau's conception of the good in social relations reflects his understanding of human nature and political society. Contrary to the British liberal tradition, Rousseauist ethics cannot be reduced to respecting others' individual rights and otherwise leaving them alone. Given man's sympathetic nature, the good society establishes institutions that cultivate that social faculty and transform it collectively into the General Will. This may lead to the "violation" of individual rights to life, liberty or property, as the whole society may decide that its interest overrides particular interests. For example, since secure private property is not possible without the conventions and protections of society, society may regulate and even expropriate private wealth for the good of the whole, without violating anyone's rights.

> The peculiar fact about this alienation is that, in taking over the goods of individuals, the community, so far from despoiling them, only assures them legitimate possession, and changes usurpation into a true right and enjoyment into proprietorship. Thus the possessors, being regarded as depositaries of public property, and having their rights respected by all the members of the State and maintained against foreign aggression by all its forces, have, by a cession which benefits both the public and still more themselves, acquired, so to speak, all that they gave up.[20]

Even the individual's life can be legitimately taken away by the state if it is in the interest of the General Will. This claim, which would shock Hobbes and Locke, is justified by Rousseau on the grounds that the individual's *human* life is dependent on society and society can therefore take it away (as in the military defense of the state or punishment for a hideous crime).

> The social treaty has for its end the preservation of the contracting parties. He who wills the end wills the means also, and the means must involve some risks, and even some losses. He who wishes to preserve his life at others' expense should also, when it is necessary, be ready to give it up for their sake. Furthermore, the citizen is no longer the judge of the dangers to which the law desires him to expose himself; and when the prince says to him: 'It is expedient for the State that you should die,' he ought to die, because it is only on that condition that he has been living in security up to the present, and because his life is no longer a mere bounty of nature, but a gift made conditionally by the State.

---

20 Rousseau, *The Social Contract* in Cole, p. 178.

The death-penalty inflicted upon criminals may be looked on in much the same light: it is in order that we may not fall victims to an assassin that we consent to die if we ourselves turn assassins. In this treaty, so far from disposing of our own lives, we think only of securing them, and it is not to be assumed that any of the parties then expects to get hanged.

Again, every malefactor, by attacking social rights, becomes on forfeit a rebel and a traitor to his country; by violating its laws he ceases to be a member of it; he even makes war upon it. In such a case the preservation of the State is inconsistent with his own, and one or the other must perish; in putting the guilty to death, we slay not so much the citizen as an enemy. The trial and the judgment are the proofs that he has broken the social treaty, and is in consequence no longer a member of the State. Since, then, he has recognized himself to be such by living there, he must be removed by exile as a violator of the compact, or by death as a public enemy; for such an enemy is not a moral person, but merely a man; and in such a case the right of war is to kill the vanquished.[21]

---

21 Rousseau, *The Social Contract* in Cole, pp. 189-190.

· 11 ·

Edmund Burke

Conservatism

Edmund Burke (1729-1797) was a British politician and political writer. Educated at Trinity College, Dublin, he moved to London in 1750. In 1766, Burke was elected to the House of Commons, where he served as a prominent member for twenty-eight years. Burke is regarded as the premier modern conservative and much of his political theory was developed as a response to the radical politics of the French Revolution.

Human Nature

Burke identifies human nature with the common faculties of reason and taste.

> On a superficial view, we may seem to differ very widely from each other in our reasonings, and no less in our pleasure: but notwithstanding this difference, which I think to be rather apparent than real, it is probable that the standard both of reason and taste is the same in all human creatures. For if there were not some principles of judgment as well as of sentiment common to all mankind, no hold could possibly be taken either on their reason or their passions, sufficient to maintain the ordinary correspondence of life. It appears indeed to be generally acknowledged, that with regard to truth and falsehood there is something fixed. We find people

in their disputes continually appealing to certain tests and standards, which are allowed on all sides, and are supposed to be established in our common nature. But there is not the same obvious concurrence in any uniform or settled principles which relate to taste.[1]

Burke devotes most of his time to discussing the human faculty of taste, or aesthetic appreciation of the beautiful.[2] He holds that men agree on basic sensations of taste and this forms a common standard for goodness.

> Let us first consider this point in the sense of taste, and the rather, as the faculty in question has taken its name from that sense. All men are agreed to call vinegar sour, honey sweet, and aloes bitter; and as they are all agreed in finding these qualities in those objects, they do not in the last differ concerning their effects with regard to pleasure and pain. They all concur in calling sweetness pleasant, and sourness and bitterness unpleasant. Here there is no diversity in their sentiments; and that there is not, appears fully from the consent of all men in the metaphors which are taken from the sense of taste. A sour temper, bitter expressions, bitter curses, a bitter fate, are terms well and strongly understood by all. And we are altogether as well understood when we say, a sweet disposition, a sweet person, a sweet condition, and the like. It is confessed, that custom and some other causes have made many deviations from the natural pleasures or pains which belong to these several tastes: but then the power of distinguishing between the natural and the acquired relish remains to the very last. A man frequently comes to prefer the taste of tobacco to that of sugar, and the flavour of vinegar to that of milk; but this makes no confusion in tastes, whilst he is sensible that the tobacco and vinegar are not sweet, and whilst he knows that habit alone has reconciled his palate to these alien pleasures.[3]

> This agreement of mankind is not confined to the taste solely. The principle of pleasure derived from sight is the same in all. Light is more pleasing than darkness. Summer, when the earth is clad in green, when the heavens are serene and bright, is more agreeable than winter, when everything makes a different appearance.[4]

However, Burke maintains that the natural human capacity for taste, appreciation of beauty and goodness, requires cultivation and development. For fully

---

1   Edmund Burke *On Taste* in Edmund Burke, *On Taste, On the Sublime and Beautiful, Reflections on the French Revolution, A Letter to a Noble Lord*, edited by Charles W. Eliot (New York, P. F. Collier & Son, 1909), p. 11.
2   Burke, *On Taste*, p. 13.
3   Burke, *On Taste*, p. 14.
4   Burke, *On Taste*, p. 15.

developed taste and judgement, the individual must have "proper and well-directed exercise" in the arts and ethics. Many do not have this and are, therefore, brutish.

> Whilst we consider taste merely according to its nature and species, we shall find its principles entirely unform; but the degree in which these principles prevail in the several individuals of mankind, is altogether as different as the principles themselves are similar. For sensibility and judgment, which are the qualities that compose what we commonly call a taste, vary exceedingly in various people. From a defect in the former of these qualities arises a want of taste; a weakness in the latter constitutes a wrong or a bad one. There are some men formed with feelings so blunt, with tempers so cold and phlegmatic, that they can hardly be said to be awake during the whole course of their lives. Upon such persons the most striking objects make but a faint and obscure impression. There are others so continually in the agitation of gross and merely sensual pleasures, or so occupied in the low drudgery of avarice, or so heated in the chase of honours and distinction, that their minds, which had been used continually to the storms of these violent and tempestuous passions, can hardly be put in motion by the delicate and refined play of the imagination. These men, though from a different cause, become as stupid and insensible as the former; but whenever either of these happen to be struck with any natural elegance or greatness, or with these qualities in any work of art, they are moved upon the same principle.
>
> The cause of a wrong taste is a defect of judgment. And this may arise from a natural weakness of understanding, (in whatever the strength of that faculty may consist), or, which is much more commonly the case, it may arise from a want of proper and well-directed exercise, which alone can make it strong and ready. Besides that ignorance, inattention, prejudice, rashness, levity, obstinacy, in short, all those passions, and all those vices, which pervert the judgment in other matters, prejudice it no less in this its more refined and elegant province.[5]

Thus, aesthetic appreciation and moral judgement are related for Burke and both require cultivation through exercise.

> ...in short, wherever the best taste differs from the worst, I am convinced that the understanding operates, and nothing else; and its operation is in reality far from being always sudden, or, when it is sudden, it is often far from being right. Men of the best taste, by consideration, come frequently to change these early and precipitate judgments, which the mind, from its aversion to neutrality and doubt, loves to form on the spot. It is known that the taste (whatever it is) is improved exactly

---

5   Burke, *On Taste*, pp. 22-23.

as we improve our judgment, by extending our knowledge, by a steady attention to our object, and by frequent exercise.[6]

And the place to gain knowledge of, and exercise in, beauty and truth is society—especially the traditions cultivated over centuries and passed down for the benefit of contemporary man.

Political Society

Burke's belief that the wisdom and beauty of the ages informs and develops our appreciation of aesthetics and goodness caused his sharp response to the French Revolution of 1789, which deliberately destroyed the past and claimed to create a new age. Burke denounced the radical changes in France during the Revolution in his most famous political work, Reflections on the French Revolution. In it, from his belief in "firm, but cautious and deliberate" change, Burke criticized the French Revolutionaries' abandonment of the past and assertion of grand theories and abstract visions of society. He insisted that the presumption of "creating" an entirely new social system based on abstract, metaphysical theories (such as Rousseau's) without reference to the social and historical circumstances in which they are applied, is to court disaster.

> But I cannot stand forward, and give praise or blame to anything which relates to human actions, and human concerns, on a simple view of the object, as it stands stripped of every relation, in all the nakedness and solitude of metaphysical abstraction. Circumstances (which with some gentlemen pass for nothing) give in reality to every political principle its distinguishing colour and discriminating effect. The circumstances are what render every civil and political scheme beneficial or noxious to mankind. Abstractedly speaking, government, as well as liberty, is good; yet could I, in common sense, ten years ago, have felicitated France on her enjoyment of a government (for she then had a government) without inquiry what the nature of that government was, or how it was administered? Can I now congratulate the same nation upon its freedom? Is it because liberty in the abstract may be classed amongst the blessings of mankind, that I am seriously to felicitate a mad-man, who has escaped from the protecting restraint and wholesome darkness of his cell, on his restoration to the enjoyment of light and liberty? Am I to congratulate a highwayman and murderer, who has broke prison, upon the recovery of his natural rights? This would be to act over again the scene of the criminals condemned

---

6   Burke, *On Taste*, p. 25.

to the galleys, and their heroic deliverer, the metaphysic knight of the sorrowful countenance.[7]

Burke objects to any "science" of politics that presumes to shape society like an experiment in physics, apart from human nature and the traditions of the past. Abstract "rights" as those found in Rousseau's *Social Contract*, pretend to establish an ideal, but only create a nightmare.

> The science of constructing a commonwealth, or renovating it, is, like every other experimental science, not to be taught a priori. Nor is it a short experience that can instruct us in that practical science: because the real effects of moral causes are not always immediate; but that which in the first instance is prejudicial may be excellent in its remoter operation; and its excellence may arise even from the ill effects it produces in the beginning. The reverse also happens: and very plausible schemes, with very pleasing commencements, have often shameful and lamentable conclusions.[8]

> The pretended rights of these theorists are all extremes: and in proportion as they are metaphysically true, they are morally and politically false.[9]

Burke, the archetypical conservative, believes that political and social change must be slow and gradual, preserving the valuable lessons and traditions of the past.

> A state without the means of some change is without the means of its conservation. Without such means it might even risk the loss of that part of the constitution which it wished the most religiously to preserve. The two principles of conservation and correction operated strongly at the two critical periods of the Restoration and Revolution, when England found itself without a king. At both those periods the nation had lost the bond of union in their ancient edifice; they did not, however, dissolve the whole fabric. On the contrary, in both cases they regenerated the deficient part of the old constitution through the parts which were not impaired. They kept these old parts exactly as they were, that the part recovered might be suited to them. They acted by the ancient organized states in the shape of their old organization, and not by the organic *moleculae* of a disbanded people. At no time, perhaps, did the sovereign legislature manifest a more tender regard

---

7   Burke, *Reflections on the French Revolution*, p. 148.
8   Burke, *Reflections on the French Revolution*, p. 198.
9   Burke, *Reflections on the French Revolution*, p. 199.

> to that fundamental principle of British constitutional policy, than at the time of the Revolution....[10]

So, Burke regarded the English Revolution of 1688 as regaining the Ancient Constitution of England and preserving the ancient liberties and traditions of the past.

> The Revolution was made to preserve our ancient, indisputable laws and liberties, and that ancient constitution of government which is our only security for law and liberty....The very idea of the fabrication of a new government is enough to fill us with disgust and horror. We wished at the period of the Revolution, and do now wish, to derive all we possess as *an inheritance from our forefathers*. Upon that body and stock of inheritance we have taken care not to inoculate any scion alien to the nature of the original plant. All the reformations we have hitherto made have proceeded upon the principle of reverence to antiquity; and I hope, nay I am persuaded, that all those which possibly may be made hereafter, will be carefully formed upon analogical precedent, authority, and example.[11]

All such English reforms, asserts Burke, were of this "organic" quality, growing from the soil of past ages and traditions, maintaining its order and dignity.

> You will observe, that from Magna Charta to the Declaration of Right, it has been the uniform policy of our constitution to claim and assert our liberties, as an *entailed inheritance* derived to us from our forefathers, and to be transmitted to our posterity; as an estate specially belonging to the people of this kingdom, without any reference whatever to any other more general or prior right. By this means our constitution preserves a unity in so great a diversity of its parts. We have an inheritable crown; an inheritable peerage; and a House of Commons and a people inheriting privileges, franchises, and liberties, from a long line of ancestors.[12]

> Through the same plan of a conformity to nature in our artificial institutions, and by calling in the aid of her unerring and powerful instincts, to fortify the fallible and feeble contrivances of our reason, we have derived several other, and those no small benefits, from considering our liberties in the light of an inheritance. Always acting as if in the presence of canonized forefathers, the spirit of freedom, leading in itself to misrule and excess, is tempered with an awful gravity. This idea of a liberal descent inspires us with a sense of habitual native dignity, which prevents that upstart insolence almost inevitably adhering to and disgracing those who are the

---

10 Burke, *Reflections on the French Revolution*, p. 161.
11 Burke, *Reflections on the French Revolution*, p. 170.
12 Burke, *Reflections on the French Revolution*, p. 172.

first acquirers of any distinction. By this means our liberty becomes a noble freedom. It carries an imposing and majestic aspect. It has a pedigree and illustrating ancestors.[13]

Reason, for Burke, must be tempered by tradition and the "Social Contract" is between the present, the past, and the future.

> Society is indeed a contract. Subordinate contracts for objects of mere occasional interest may be dissolved at pleasure-but the state ought not to be considered as nothing better than a partnership agreement in a trade of pepper and coffee, calico or tobacco, or some other such low concern, to be taken up for a little temporary interest, and to be dissolved by the fancy of the parties. It is to be looked on with other reverence; because it is not a partnership in things subservient only to the gross animal existence of a temporary and perishable nature. It is a partnership in all science; a partnership in all art; a partnership in every virtue, and in all perfection. As the ends of such a partnership cannot be obtained in many generations, it becomes a partnership not only between those who are living, but between those who are living, those who are dead, and those who are to be born. Each contract of each particular state is but a clause in the great primaeval contract of eternal society, linking the lower with the higher natures, connecting the visible and invisible world, according to a fixed compact sanctioned by the inviolable oath which holds all physical and all moral natures, each in their appointed place.[14]

A radical disregard for tradition and affinity for "innovation" for its own sake, Burke considers typical of a mean spirit and ignorant mind.

> A spirit of innovation is generally the result of a selfish temper, and confined views. People will not look forward to posterity, who never look backward to their ancestors.[15]

Social Ethics

The standard of individual and social goodness for the conservative Burke is cultivated taste and judgement and those social institutions that foster them. A good person will respect tradition and authority; a good society will value the religion, education and property which cultivates such people.

---

13 Burke, *Reflections on the French Revolution*, p. 173.
14 *Reflections on the French Revolution*, pp. 232-233.
15 *Reflections on the French Revolution*, p. 170.

All good things in England come from the tradition of the English gentleman and religion. These exude "moderation, discretion and stability."[16]

> Nothing is more certain, than that our manners, our civilization, and all the good things which are connected with manners and with civilization, have, in this European world of ours, depended for ages upon two principles; and were indeed the result of both combined; I mean the spirit of a gentleman, and the spirit of religion. The nobility and the clergy, the one by profession, the other by patronage, kept learning in existence, even in the midst of arms and confusions....[17]

Burke contrasts the civility of English rulers with the "coarseness and vulgarity"[18] of the leaders of the French Revolution.

> On the scheme of this barbarous philosophy, which is the offspring of cold hearts and muddy understandings, and which is as void of solid wisdom as it is destitute of all taste and elegance, laws are to be supported only by their own terrors, and by the concern which each individual may find in them from his own private speculations, or can spare to them from his own private interests. In the *groves* of their academy, at the end of every vista, you see nothing but the gallows.[19]

Thus, for Burke, goodness comes from a certain breeding in the beauty and traditions of the past. He is less interested in vague notions of "liberty" or "rights" than in their results.

> Flattery corrupts both the receiver and the giver; and adulation is not of more service to the people than to kings. I should therefore suspend my congratulations on the new liberty of France, until I was informed how it had been combined with government; with public force; with the discipline and obedience of armies; with the collection of an effective and welldistributed revenue; with morality and religion; with the solidity of property; with peace and order; with civil and social manners. All these (in their way) are good things too; and, without them, liberty is not a benefit whilst it lasts, and is not likely to continue long. The effect of liberty to individuals is that they may do what they please: we ought to see what it will please them to do, before we risk congratulations....[20]

---

16   Burke, *Reflections on the French Revolution*, p. 181.
17   Burke, *Reflections on the French Revolution*, p. 215.
18   Burke, *Reflections on the French Revolution*, p. 216.
19   Burke, *Reflections on the French Revolution*, p. 214.
20   Burke, *Reflections on the French Revolution*, pp. 148-149.

A good society, for Burke, will cultivate citizens of "moderation, discretion and stability" and preserve the institutions of nobility, private property and the Church. Burke was a practicing Anglican and staunch believer in the established Church of England. He attributed England's decency and civility to its religion and was appalled at the French destruction of its Church.

> We know, and what is better, we feel inwardly, that religion is the basis of civil society, and the source of all good and of all comfort. In England we are so convinced of this, that there is no rust of superstition, with which the accumulated absurdity of the human mind might have crusted it over in the course of ages, that ninety-nine in a hundred of the people of England would not prefer to impiety.[21]

> We know, and it is our pride to know, that man is by his constitution a religious animal; that atheism is against, not only our reason, but our instincts; and that it cannot prevail long. But if, in the moment of riot, and in a drunken delirium from the hot spirit drawn out of the alembic of hell, which in France is now so furiously boiling, we should uncover our nakedness, by throwing off that Christian religion which has hitherto been our boast and comfort, and one great source of civilization amongst us, and amongst many other nations, we are apprehensive (being well aware that the mind will not endure a void) that some uncouth, pernicious, and degrading superstition might take place of it.[22]

Burke remains the archetypical modern conservative and his emphasis on traditional values, on order and stability, on property, God and the State, reappear whenever the Western world goes through a conservative period.

---

21 Burke, *Reflections on the French Revolution*, p. 226.
22 Burke, *Reflections on the French Revolution*, p. 227.

· 12 ·

John Stuart Mill

Intellectual Liberty

John Stuart Mill (1806-1873) was an English philosopher who brought traditional British liberalism into the nineteenth century and showed its usefulness to a developing British society. His father James had been a prominent Political Economist and Utilitarian philosopher; he taught John Stuart Greek at the age of three and Latin at the age of eight, completing a full classical education at the age of fourteen, after which John Stuart had a nervous breakdown. He worked for the East India Company from 1823 until 1856 and served in Parliament from 1865 to 1868. Mill wrote in Political Economy, Ethics and Logic as well as Political Theory.

Human Nature

J. S. Mill accepted the basic liberal view of man as an independent, material being, but modified it with a "social feeling" that causes individuals to have sympathy for others' sufferings and regard their interests as our own.

> The social state is at once so natural, so necessary, and so habitual to man, that, except in some unusual circumstances or by an effort of voluntary abstraction, he never conceives himself otherwise than as a member of a body; and this association

is riveted more and more, as mankind are further removed from the state of savage independence.[1]

They are also familiar with the fact of co-operating with others and proposing to themselves a collective, not an individual interest as the aim (at least for the time being) of their actions. So long as they are co-operating, their ends are identified with those of others; there is at least a temporary feeling that the interests of others are their own interests. Not only does all strengthening of social ties, and all healthy growth of society, give to each individual a stronger personal interest in practically consulting the welfare of others; it also leads him to identify his *feelings* more and more with their good, or at least with an even greater degree of practical consideration for it. He comes, as though instinctively, to be conscious of himself as a being who of course pays regard to others. The good of others becomes to him a thing naturally and necessarily to be attended to, like any of the physical conditions of our existence. Now, whatever amount of this feeling a person has, he is urged by the strongest motives both of interest and of sympathy to demonstrate it....[2]

So, while Mill certainly considers man a free individual (especially in conscience and intellect), he regards him also as naturally social by virtue of his sympathetic qualities.[3]

...a person in whom the social feeling is at all developed, can not bring himself to think of the rest of his fellow-creatures as struggling rivals with him for the means of happiness, whom he must desire to see defeated in their object in order that he may succeed in his. The deeply rooted conception which every individual even now has of himself as a social being, tends to make him feel it one of his natural wants that there should be harmony between his feelings and aims and those of his fellow-creatures.[4]

These social "feelings" in man are more pronounced as civilization progresses and becomes the basis for social harmony and ethics.

Human beings, on this point, only differ from other animals in two particulars. First, in being capable of sympathising, not solely with their offspring, or, like some of the more noble animals, with some superior animal who is kind to them, but

---

1 John Stuart Mill, *Utilitarianism, On Liberty*, and *Considerations on Representative Government*, edited by H. B. Acton (New York, Dent Dutton, 1976), p. 29.
2 Mill, *Utilitarianism*, p. 30.
3 Mill, *Utilitarianism*, p. 132.
4 Mill, *Utilitarianism*, p. 31.

with all human, and even with all sentient, beings. Secondly, in having a more developed intelligence, which gives a wider range to the whole of their sentiments, whether self-regarding or sympathetic. By virtue of his superior intelligence, even apart from his superior range of sympathy, a human being is capable of apprehending a community of interest between himself and the human society of which he forms a part, such that any conduct which threatens the security of the society generally, is threatening to his own, and calls forth his instinct (if instinct it be) of self-defence. The same superiority of intelligence, joined to the power of sympathising with human beings generally, enables him to attach himself to the collective idea of his tribe, his country, or mankind, in such a manner that any act hurtful to them rouses his instinct of sympathy, and urges him to resistance....

This sentiment, in itself, has nothing moral in it; what is moral is, the exclusive subordination of it to the social sympathies, so as to wait on and obey their call. For the natural feeling tends to make us resent indiscriminately whatever any one does that is disagreeable to us; but when moralised by the social feeling, it only acts in the directions conformable to the general good....[5]

The way in which this "social feeling" is developed in the individual is through education, which, for Mill, requires a certain kind of political society.

Political Society

The development of man's social sympathy requires a tolerant, liberal education; and that, for Mill, necessitates individual liberty. By "liberty," Mill means the freedom to believe and express all manner of ideas. Such freedom of expression must not be suppressed by political, ecclesiastical or social forces. For Mill, the last, social convention and prejudice, are the most dangerous to individual intellectual liberty.

> ...when society is itself the tyrant—society collectively over the separate individuals who compose it—its means of tyrannising are not restricted to the act which it may do by the hands of its political functionaries. Society can and does execute its own mandates: and if it issues wrong mandates instead of right, or any mandates at all in things with which it ought not to meddle, it practises a social tyranny more formidable than many kinds of political oppression, since, though not usually upheld by such extreme penalties, it leaves fewer means of escape, penetrating much more deeply into the details of life, and enslaving the soul itself. Protection, therefore, against the tyranny of the magistrate is not enough: there needs protection also

---

5   Mill, *Utilitarianism*, p. 48.

against the tyranny of the prevailing opinion and feeling; against the tendency of society to impose, by other means than civil penalties, its own ideas and practices as rules of conduct on those who dissent from them; to fetter the development, and, if possible, prevent the formation, of any individuality not in harmony with its ways, and compels all characters to fashion themselves upon the model of its own. There is a limit to the legitimate interference of collective opinion with individual independence....[6]

For Mill, human progress requires absolute liberty of conscience, belief and expression.[7] Such liberty, from government censorship and social prejudice, will create a free marketplace of ideas—the debate of which will enhance truth and social progress.

This, then, is the appropriate region of human liberty. It comprises, first, the inward domain of consciousness; demanding liberty of conscience in the most comprehensive sense; liberty of thought and feeling; absolute freedom of opinion and sentiment on all subjects, practical or speculative, scientific, moral, or theological. The liberty of expressing and publishing opinions may seem to fall under a different principle, since it belongs to that part of the conduct of an individual which concerns other people; but, being almost of as much importance as the liberty of thought itself, and resting in great part on the same reasons, is practically inseparable from it. Secondly, the principle requires liberty of tastes and pursuits; of framing the plan of our life to suit our own character; of doing as we like, subject to such consequences as may follow: without impediment from our fellow-creatures, so long as what we do does not harm them, even though they should think our conduct foolish, perverse, or wrong. Thirdly, from this liberty of each individual, follows the liberty, within the same limits of combination among individuals; freedom to unite, for any purpose not involving harm to others: the persons combining being supposed to be of full age, and not forced or deceived.[8]

Mill gives two arguments for liberty of expression in the service of truth: (1) the dissenting opinion may be true and its suppression would rob mankind of useful knowledge and (2) even if the opinion is false, it will strengthen the correct view by challenging it.

But the peculiar evil of silencing the expression of an opinion is, that it is robbing the human race; posterity as well as the existing generation; those who dissent from the opinion, still more than those who hold it. If the opinion is right, they

---

6   Mill, *On Liberty*, p. 68.
7   Mill, *On Liberty*, p. 74.
8   Mill, *On Liberty*, p. 75.

are deprived of the opportunity of exchanging error for truth: if wrong, they lose, what is almost as great a benefit, the clearer perception and livelier impression of truth, produced by its collision with error.

It is necessary to consider separately these two hypotheses, each of which has a distinct branch of the argument corresponding to it. We can never be sure that the opinion we are endeavouring to stifle is a false opinion; and if we were sure, stifling it would be an evil still.[9]

So, incorrect opinions serve the valuable purpose of continually sharpening correct views.

He who knows only his own side of the case, knows little of that. His reasons may be good, and no one may have been able to refute them. But if he is equally unable to refute the reasons on the opposite side; if he does not so much as know what they are, he has no ground for preferring either opinion....He must be able to hear them from persons who actually believe them; who defend them in earnest, and do their very utmost for them. He must know them in their most plausible and persuasive form; he must feel the whole force of the difficulty which the true view of the subject has to encounter and dispose of; else he will never really possess himself of the portion of truth which meets and removes that difficulty.[10]

Such free debate will enhance social progress and human happiness.

To discover to the world something which deeply concerns it, and of which it was previously ignorant; to prove to it that it had been mistaken on some vital point of temporal or spiritual interest, is as important a service as a human being can render to his fellow-creatures....[11]

Of course, Mill did not extend the liberty of thought and expression to the liberty of *action*, which society has a right to curtail, if it harms the rights of others or disturbs social peace.

Such being the reasons which make it imperative that human beings should be free to form opinions, and to express their opinions without reserve; and such the baneful consequences to the intellectual, and through that to the moral nature of man, unless this liberty is either conceded, or asserted in spite of prohibition; let us next examine whether the same reasons do not require that men should be free to

---

9   Mill, *On Liberty*, p. 79.
10 Mill, *On Liberty*, p. 97.
11 Mill, *On Liberty*, p. 89.

act upon their opinions—to carry these out in their lives, without hindrance, either physical or moral, from their fellow-men, so long as it is at their own risk and peril. This last proviso is of course indispensable. No one pretends that actions should be as free as opinions. On the contrary, even opinions lose their immunity when the circumstances in which they are expressed are such as to constitute their expression a positive instigation to some mischievous act. An opinion that corn-dealers are starvers of the poor, or that private property is robbery, ought to be unmolested when simply circulated through the press, but may justly incur punishment when delivered orally to an excited mob assembled before the house of a corn-dealer, or when handed about among the same mob in the form of a placard.[12]

This qualification of Mill's liberty, to limit freedom of action and even speech that can provoke public upheaval, becomes the basis for American "freedom of speech" guaranteed by the First Amendment, so long as there is no "clear and present danger" that violent speech may lead to violent action. Or, as Mill puts it, simply:

The liberty of the individual must be thus far limited; he must not make himself a nuisance to other people.[13]

As to the institutions of government that will serve man's moral and intellectual progress best, Mill advises a state based in popular will which will improve man's social faculties.

There is no difficulty in showing that the ideally best form of government is that in which the sovereignty, or supreme controlling power in the last resort, is vested in the entire aggregate of the community; every citizen not only having a voice in the exercise of that ultimate sovereignty, but being, at least occasionally, called on to take an actual part in the government, by the personal discharge of some public function, local or general.

To test this proposition, it has to be examined in reference to the two branches into which...the inquiry into the goodness of a government conveniently divided itself, namely, how far it promotes the good management of the affairs of society by means of the existing faculties, moral, intellectual, and active, of its various members, and what is its effect in improving or deteriorating those faculties.[14]

---

12 Mill, *On Liberty*, p. 114.
13 Mill, *On Liberty*, p. 114.
14 Mill, *Considerations on Representative Government*, pp. 207–208.

In a large, modern country, where it is impossible for every citizen to participate directly in governing, Mill advocates a representative democracy. However, he does not suggest giving equal votes to everyone; rather, he believes in a "plurality" or extra votes for citizens of superior intellectual ability. This will make for a wiser, more tolerant society.

> The only thing which can justify reckoning one person's opinion as equivalent to more than one is individual mental superiority; and what is wanted is some approximate means of ascertaining that. If there existed such a thing as a really national education or a trustworthy system of general examination, education might be tested directly. In the absence of these, the nature of a person's occupation is some test. An employer of labour is on the average more intelligent than a labourer; for he must labour with his head, and not solely with his hands. A foreman is generally more intelligent than an ordinary labourer, and a labourer in the skilled trades than in the unskilled. A banker, merchant, or manufacturer is likely to be more intelligent than a tradesman, because he has larger and more complicated interests to manage. In all these cases it is not the having merely undertaken the superior function, but the successful performance of it, that tests the qualifications; for which reason, as well as to prevent persons from engaging nominally in an occupation for the sake of the vote, it would be proper to require that the occupation should have been persevered in for some length of time (say three years). Subject to some such condition, two or more votes might be allowed to every person who exercises any of these superior functions. The liberal professions, when really and not nominally practised, imply, of course, a still higher degree of instruction; and wherever a sufficient examination, or any serious conditions of education, are required before entering on a profession, its members could be admitted at once to a plurality of votes. The same rule might be applied to graduates of universities; and even to those who bring satisfactory certificates of having passed through the course of study required by any school at which the higher branches of knowledge are taught, under proper securities that the teaching is real, and not a mere pretense. The "local" or "middle class" examination for the degree of Associate, so laudably and public-spiritedly established by the Universities of Oxford and Cambridge, and any similar ones which may be instituted by other competent bodies (provided they are fairly open to all comers), afford a ground on which plurality of votes might with great advantage be accorded to those who have passed the test.[15]

And, at a time when it was considered very radical, Mill advocated allowing women to vote.

---

15 Mill, *Considerations on Representative Government*, pp. 285–286.

> In the preceding argument for universal, but graduated suffrage, I have taken no account of difference of sex. I consider it to be as entirely irrelevant to political rights as difference in height or in the colour of the hair. All human beings have the same interest in good government; the welfare of all is alike affected by it, and they have equal need of a voice in it to secure their share in its benefits. If there be any difference, women require it more than men, since, being physically weaker, they are more dependent on law and society for protection. Mankind have long since abandoned the only premise which will support the conclusion that women ought not to have votes. No one now holds that women should be in personal servitude; that they should have no thought, wish, or occupation, but to be the domestic drudges of husbands, fathers, or brothers.[16]

Social Ethics

John Stuart Mill was a Utilitarian. Utilitarianism asserts that the good is pleasure and pleasure is happiness. Social good, therefore, is the "greatest good for the greatest number." It is an ethical system that grows naturally from Locke's view of man as a sensory, material being desirous of "life, liberty, and property." Mill, however, developed the hedonistic utilitarianism of Bentham by distinguishing higher and lower pleasures. Greater human pleasure may not simply mean an increase in the *quantity* of goods, but also an increase in the *quality* of goods enjoyed. For Mill, intellectual and moral pleasures are higher than the base physical pleasures we share with the beasts.

> The creed which accepts as the foundation of morals, Utility, or the Greatest Happiness Principle, holds that actions are right in proportion as they tend to promote happiness, wrong as they tend to produce the reverse of happiness. By happiness is intended pleasure, and the absence of pain; by unhappiness, pain, and the privation of pleasure.[17]

> But there is no known Epicurean theory of life which does not assign to the pleasures of the intellect, of the feelings and imagination, and of the moral sentiments, a much higher value as pleasures than to those of mere sensation.[18]

---

16 Mill, *Considerations on Representative Government*, p. 290.
17 Mill, *Utilitarianism*, p. 6.
18 Mill, *Utilitarianism*, p. 7.

It would be absurd that while, in estimating all other things, quality is considered as well as quantity, the estimation of pleasures should be supposed to depend on quantity alone.[19]

It is better to be a human being dissatisfied than a pig satisfied; better to be Socrates, dissatisfied than a fool satisfied.[20]

John Stuart Mill's modification of liberal psychology to include a social aspect and his development of utilitarianism to include quality as well as quantity, effectively brought British liberalism into the nineteenth and twentieth centuries. His arguments for liberty greatly affected freedom of expression in England and America, and his advocacy of extending the right to vote greatly influenced English politics of the late 1800's. His emphasis on knowledge through debate and progress through knowledge underlies contemporary Western civilization.

---

19 Mill, *Utilitarianism*, p. 7.
20 Mill, *Utilitarianism*, p. 9.

· 13 ·

Karl Marx

Communism

Karl Marx (1818-1883) was a German philosopher and economist and the Father of modern Communism. He came from a family of learned, rabbinical Jews, though his father converted to Protestant Christianity in order to be allowed to enter the legal profession. Marx studied at the University of Berlin and took a Ph.D. in Philosophy from the University of Jena. He served as the editor of various radical newspapers in Germany and France, for which he was expelled from both countries. He eventually settled in London, where he remained the rest of his life. The Communist countries of the contemporary world (the Soviet Union, the People's Republic of China, etc.) trace their political and economic systems to Marx's ideas, as do Communist Parties around the world (including, in America, the Communist Party of the United States of America, or C.P.U.S.A.).

Human Nature

Marx regarded man's unique nature (or "species-being") as his distinctive ability to produce his own material environment and "objectify" his personality in the world through creative activity.

> Men can be distinguished from animals by consciousness, by religion, or anything else you like. They themselves begin to distinguish themselves from animals as soon as they begin to produce their means of subsistence, a step which is conditioned by their physical organization. By producing their means of subsistence men are indirectly producing their actual material life.[1]

Human production, for Marx, is not merely creating the necessities of life; it is also an expression of man's unique nature and an activity through which he knows himself by shaping the world and seeing himself in it. People literally are *what* (and how) they *produce*.

> The way in which men produce their means of subsistence depends first of all on the nature of the actual means of subsistence they find in existence and have to reproduce. This mode of production must not be considered simply as being the production of the physical existence of the individuals. Rather it is a definite form of activity of these individuals, a definite form of expressing their life, a definite mode of life on their part. As individuals express their life, so they are. What they are, therefore, coincides with their production, both with *what* they produce and with *how* they produce. The nature of individuals thus depends on the material conditions determining their production.[2]

Therefore, for Marx, man does not have a fixed, constant nature, since it is conditioned by the way in which he produces during different times in history and in different societies. All humans have the capacity to produce, but they do so differently in different social conditions. Ideally, man's production is creative and self-expressing, so that he sees his own unique personality in his product and his potential is realized. For Marx, such fully human production is possible only in Communism.

> Thus it is in the working over the objective world that man first really affirms himself as a species-being. This production is his active species-life. Through it nature appears as his work and his reality. The object of work is therefore the objectification of the species-life of man; for he duplicates himself not only intellectually, in his mind, but also actively in reality and thus can look at his image in a world he has created.[3]

---

1 Karl Marx, *The German Ideology* in *Karl Marx: Selected Writings*, edited by David McLellan (New York, Oxford University Press, 1978), p. 160.
2 Marx, p. 161.
3 Karl Marx, *Economic and Philosophic Manuscripts* in McLellan, p. 82.

Just as God, in the Book of Genesis, creates the world, and man in His own image, man, for Marx, creates his own world and sees his image in his creation. The power and control over destiny that the Judeo-Christian tradition identifies with God, Marx identifies with man.

The problem, for Marx, is that capitalism prevents man from realizing his creative potential. Rather than controlling nature and his destiny, man in capitalist society is controlled by forces beyond his reach. Rather than objectifying his subjectivity in the world he creates, man in capitalist society is manipulated by production and alienated.

Under capitalism, for Marx, man is alienated in four ways: (1) from the object of his production (over which he has no control); (2) from his subjectivity (as a creative being-confirmed by that object); (3) from nature and society (which he should control, but which controls him); and (4) from other people (with whom he should cooperate to control nature, but instead competes with for work, wealth, prestige, etc.).[4]

The revolutionary overthrowing of capitalism and the establishment of communism will, for Marx, free people from all these forms of alienation and allow them to realize their true nature ("species-being") by collectively objectifying their subjectivity. Perfect freedom and harmony will be realized.

> ...there is communism as the positive abolition of private property and thus of human self-alienation and therefore the real reappropriation of the human essence by and for man. This is communism as the complete and conscious return of man conserving all the riches of previous development for man himself as a social, i.e. human being. Communism as completed naturalism is humanism and as completed humanism is naturalism. It is the genuine solution of the antagonism between man and nature and between man and man. It is the true solution of the struggle between existence and essence, between objectification and self-affirmation, between freedom and necessity, between individual and species. It is the solution to the riddle of history and knows itself to be this solution.[5]

> The supersession of private property is therefore the complete emancipation of all human senses and qualities, but it is this emancipation precisely in that these senses and qualities have become human, both subjectively and objectively. The eye has become a human eye when its object has become a social, human object produced by man and destined for him.[6]

---

4   Marx, *Economic and Philosophic Manuscripts*, pp. 81-83.
5   Marx, *Economic and Philosophic Manuscripts*, p. 89.
6   Marx, *Economic and Philosophic Manuscripts*, p. 92.

In Communist society, according to Marx, the State (with the help of highly advanced technology) will take care of the general production, liberating individuals to produce and create in a wide range of activities.

> For as soon as the distribution of labour comes into being, each man has a particular, exclusive sphere of activity, which is forced upon him and from which he cannot escape. He is a hunter, a fisherman, a shepherd, or a critical critic, and must remain so if he does not want to lose his means of livelihood; while in communist society, where nobody has one exclusive sphere of activity but each can become accomplished in any branch he wishes, society regulates the general production and thus makes it possible for me to do one thing today and another tomorrow, to hunt in the morning, fish in the afternoon, rear cattle in the evening, criticize after dinner, just as I have a mind, without ever becoming hunter, fisherman, cowherd, or critic.[7]

So, the vision of Communist society for Marx, and subsequent Marxists, is a place where people are liberated from oppressive, alienated work and toil by technology and a new social organization and freed to be creative in a variety of activities and realize their true potential and fulfillment. For Christians, this sounds a little like the Kingdom of Heaven, but for the atheist Marx, it is possible here on earth.

Political Society

The road to the perfect society of Communism is a long historical journey through many unhappy eras, ending in capitalism. Because mankind if distinguished, for Marx, by his productive capacity, history is seen as the development of that capacity through different social and economic systems. Therefore, the way in which people *produce* is the most important aspect of their lives, from which all other aspects are derived. Marx sees the economic system of any society as the real foundation of civilization and the legal, political, religious, moral, academic, aesthetic and philosophical dimensions of society as ideological reflections of that economic reality.

> The production of ideas, of conceptions, of consciousness, is at first directly interwoven with the material activity and the material intercourse of men, the language of real life. Conceiving, thinking, the mental intercourse of men, appear at this stage as the direct efflux of their material behaviour. The same applies to

---

7   Marx, *The German Ideology*, p. 161.

mental production as expressed in the language of politics, laws, morality, religion, metaphysics, etc. of a people. Men are the producers of their conceptions, ideas, etc.—real, active men, as they are conditioned by a definite development of their productive forces and of the intercourse corresponding to these, up to its furthest forms. Consciousness can never be anything else than conscious existence, and the existence of men is the actual life-process. If in all ideology men and their circumstances appear upside-down as in a *camera obscura*, this phenomenon arises just as much from their historical lifeprocess as the inversion of objects on the retina does from their physical life-process....we do not set out from what men say, imagine, conceive, nor from men as narrated, thought of, imagined, conceived, in order to arrive at men in the flesh.

We set out from real, active men, and on the basis of their real life-process we demonstrate the development of the ideological reflexes and echoes of this life-process. The phantoms formed in the human brain are also, necessarily, sublimates of their material life-process, which is empirically verifiable and bound to material premises. Morality, religion, metaphysics, all the rest of ideology and their corresponding forms of consciousness, thus no longer retain the semblance of independence. They have no history, no development; but men, developing their material production and their material inter course, alter, along with this their real existence, their thinking and the products of their thinking. Life is not determined by consciousness, but consciousness by life.[8]

In the social production of their life, men enter into definite relations that are indispensable and independent of their will, relations of production which correspond to a definite stage of development of their material productive forces. The sum total of these relations of production constitutes the economic structure of society, the real foundation, on which rises a legal and political superstructure and to which correspond definite forms of social consciousness. The mode of production of material life conditions the social, political, and intellectual life process in general. It is not the consciousness of men that determines their being, but, on the contrary, their social being that determines their consciousness.[9]

To display this Marxian materialism in a simple way, the economic system of a society (including forces and relations of production) influence all the other aspects of society, especially thought.

Thus, ideas or thoughts are conditioned by the way in which people work; they do not have an independent existence.

---

8   Marx, *The German Ideology*, p. 164.
9   Marx, Preface to *A Critique of Political Economy* in McLellan, p. 389.

> Hitherto men have constantly made up for themselves false conceptions about themselves, about what they are and what they ought to be. They have arranged their relationships according to their ideas of God, of normal man, etc. The phantoms of their brains have got out of their hands....
>
> The premises from which we begin are not arbitrary ones, not dogmas, but real premises from which abstraction can only be made in the imagination. They are the real individuals, their activity and the material conditions under which they live, both those which they find already existing and those produced by their activity. These premises can thus be verified in a purely empirical way.[10]

So, for example, Marxism materialism sees artistic achievement as affected by the economic system in which it arises.

> Sancho imagines that Raphael produced his pictures independently of the division of labour that existed in Rome at the time. If he were to compare Raphael with Leonardo da Vinci and Titian, he would know how greatly Raphael's works of art depended on the flourishing of Rome at that time, which occurred under Florentine influence, while the works of Leonardo depended on the state of things in Florence, and the works of Titian, at a later period, depended on the totally different development of Venice. Raphael as much as any other artist was determined by the technical advances in art made before him, by the organization of society and the division of labour in his locality, and, finally, by the division of labour in all the countries with which his locality had intercourse. Whether an individual like Raphael succeeds in developing his talent depends wholly on demand, which in turn depends on the division of labour and the conditions of human culture resulting from it.[11]

Also, religion, for Marx, merely reflects and reinforces the socioeconomic structures of a given period in history.

> The religious world is but the reflex of the real world. And for a society based upon the production of commodities, in which the producers in general enter into social relations with one another by treating their products as commodities and values, whereby they reduce their individual private labour to the standard of homogeneous human labour—for such a society, Christianity with its *cultus* of abstract man, more especially in its bourgeois developments, Protestantism, Deism, etc., is the most fitting form of religion. In the ancient Asiatic and other ancient modes of production, we find that the conversion of products into commodities, holds a

---

10 Marx, *The German Ideology*, pp. 159-160.
11 Marx, *The German Ideology*, p. 189.

subordinate place, which, however, increases in importance as the primitive communities approach nearer and nearer to their dissolution. Trading nations, properly so called, exist in the ancient world only in its interstices, like the gods of Epicurus in the Intermundia, or like Jews in the pores of Polish society. Those ancient social organisms of production are, as compared with bourgeois society, extremely simple and transparent. But they are founded either on the immature development of man individually, who has not yet severed the umbilical cord that unites him with his fellowmen in a primitive tribal community, or upon direct relations of subjection. They can arise and exist only when the development of the productive power of labour has not risen beyond a low stage, and when, therefore, the social relations within the sphere of material life, between man and man, and between man and Nature, are correspondingly narrow. This narrowness is reflected in the ancient worship of Nature, and in the other elements of the popular religions. The religious reflex of the real world can, in any case, only then finally vanish, when the practical relations of everyday life offer to man none but perfectly intelligible and reasonable relations with regard to his fellowmen and to Nature.[12]

And politics, for Marx, reflects the dominant mode of production and more directly than anything else: governments are the "executive committee" of the ruling economic class, as he asserts in *The Communist Manifesto*:

Each step in the development of the bourgeoisie was accompanied by a corresponding political advance of that class. An oppressed class under the sway of the feudal nobility, an armed and self-governing association in the medieval commune; here independent urban republic (as in Italy and Germany), there taxable 'third estate' of the monarchy (as in France), afterwards, in the period of manufacture proper, serving either the semi-feudal or the absolute monarchy as a counterpoise against the nobility, and, in fact, corner-stone of the great monarchies in general, the bourgeoisie has at last, since the establishment of Modern Industry and of the world-market, conquered for itself, in the modern representative State, exclusive political sway. The executive of the modern State is but a committee for managing the common affairs of the whole bourgeoisie.[13]

Political theory, therefore, merely enshrines prevailing economic values.

The ideas of the ruling class are in every epoch the ruling ideas, i.e., the class which is the ruling material force of society is at the same time its ruling intellectual force. The class which has the means of material production at its disposal, has control at the same time over the means of mental production, so that thereby, generally

---

12 Marx, *Capital*, Vol. I, in McLellan, p. 441.
13 Marx, *The Communist Manifesto* in McLellan, p. 223.

speaking, the ideas of those who lack the means of mental production are subject to it. The ruling ideas are nothing more than the ideal expression of the dominant material relationships, the dominant material relationships grasped as ideas; hence of the relationships which make the one class the ruling one, therefore, the ideas of its dominance.[14]

Thus, for Marx, all thought and systems of ideas are conditioned by the historical economic relations of society. History is not shaped by ideas, but by technological forces, which ideas then reflect and explain. And, because technology advances, mankind's ideas also change and advance. The "forces of production," as Marx calls technology, allow man to gain ever greater control over nature. But, each method of production creates specific social "relations of production" involving distinct classes and customs and ideas.[15]

MODE OF PRODUCTION	Primitive Communism (tribal)	Antiquity (Greek & Roman)	Feudalism (Medieval Europe)	Capitalism (Industrialism)	Socialism	Communism
RELATIONS OF PRODUCTION	Ruling Class	MASTER	LANDLORDS	BOURGEOISIE	PROLETARIAT	–
	Working Class	SLAVE	PEASANTS	PROLETARIAT	PROLETARIAT	–

For Marx, while each mode of production or historical stage gives rise to a certain class structure, the development of technology renders that social organization obsolete. This disjuncture between advancing technology and established social structures eventually causes a revolution forcing social relations to conform with the new productive forces.

> At a certain stage of their development, the material productive forces of society come in conflict with the existing relations of production, or—what is but a legal expression for the same thing—with the property relations within which they have been at work hitherto. From forms of development of the productive forces these relations turn into their fetters. Then begins an epoch of social revolution. With the change of the economic foundations, the entire immense superstructure is more or less rapidly transformed. In considering such transformations a distinction should always be made between the material transformation of the economic

---

14 Marx, *The German Ideology*, p. 176.
15 Marx, *Selected Writings* in McLellan, pp. 389–390, 222, 161–165.

conditions of production, which can be determined with the precision of natural science, and the legal, political, religious, aesthetic, or philosophic-in short, ideological forms in which men become conscious of this conflict and fight it out. Just as our opinion of an individual is not based on what he thinks of himself, so can we not judge of such a period of transformation by its own consciousness; on the contrary, this consciousness must be explained rather from the contradictions of material life, from the existing conflict between the social productive forces and the relations of production.[16]

Marx emphasizes that these historical social revolutions are usually fought out in the realm of the "superstructure" or political ideology (e.g., feudal monarchy versus capitalist democracy) and religious controversy (Medieval Catholicism versus Modern Protestantism). But the origins of these philosophical disputes are *economic* and are merely framed in the language of law, politics and religion. All "ideology," for Marx, must be understood in terms of its class basis. For example, Marxists see St. Thomas Aquinas' emphasis on hierarchy as merely reflecting the class structure of the Middle Ages, and John Locke's emphasis on liberty and equality as merely reflecting emerging capitalism. So, in explaining both social change and philosophical disputes, Marx advises examining the economic conditions.

Marx's most detailed exposition on historical change concerns that present in his own time: the revolution that ends capitalism and propels society into socialism. The source of this change is the "contradiction" in capitalism between the increasingly *social* "forces of production" (large scale industrial production) and the *private* "relations of production" (private ownership of the means of production). This contradiction is represented in the conflict between the owning class (bourgeoisie) and the working class (proletariat), which eventually causes a revolution that brings the relations of production into conformity with the forces of production. And that is socialism.

Marxist Economics and Socialist Revolution

The specific catalyst for a working class socialist revolution is what Marx called a capitalist "crisis of overproduction." This is what we might call a "depression" or severe "recession" and is characterized by reduced industrial production, high unemployment and poverty. Such a crisis, for Marx, reflects the contradiction between the social "forces of production" and the private "relations of

---

16 Marx, Preface to *A Critique of Political Economy*, pp. 389-390.

production." Therefore, these economic crises, and all their human misery, are endemic to capitalism and will plague mankind until capitalism is overthrown and replaced by socialism. Socialism will bring the social relations of production into conformity with the social forces of production and all economic problems will end. After a brief "dictatorship of the proletariat" during the socialist stage of history, the state will "wither away" as the era of perfect harmony and freedom of communism is reached.

The capitalist "crisis of overproduction" that ushers in socialism occurs during the low period of the Business Cycle. The Business Cycle is what economists call the uneven growth or "boom and bust" cycle of a capitalist economy. Over time, market economics grow in an up-and-down fashion. The boom period is marked by increased production, low unemployment and prosperity. The bust period is characterized by lower sales, decreased levels of production and high unemployment and poverty. Why does a capitalist economy go through these ups and downs? Marx's answer justified a revolution.

Marx called the "bust" or "depression" in a capitalist economy a "crisis of *overproduction*" because the unemployment and poverty of this period is accompanied by an *overabundance* of unsold goods. During a capitalist depression people are out of work and poor not because there are too *few* goods, but because there are too *many* goods. This absurdity of poverty in the midst of plenty tells us that there is something fundamentally wrong with the capitalist mode of production. As Marx explains in the *Communist Manifesto*:

> Modern bourgeois society with its relations of production, of exchange and of property, a society that has conjured up such gigantic means of production and of exchange, is like the sorcerer, who is no longer able to control the powers of the nether world which he called up by his spells. The history of industry and commerce for many a decade past is but the history of the revolt of modern productive forces against modern conditions of production, against the property relations that are the conditions for the existence of the bourgeoisie and of its rule. It is enough to mention the commercial crises that by their periodical return put on trial, each time more threateningly, the existence of the entire bourgeois society. In these crises a great part not only of the existing products, but also of the previously create productive forces, are periodically destroyed. In these crises there breaks out an epidemic that, in all earlier epochs, would have seemed an absurdity-the epidemic of over-production. Society suddenly finds itself put back into a state of momentary barbarism; it appears as if a famine, a universal war of devastation, has cut off the supply of every means of subsistence; industry and commerce seem to be

destroyed; and why? Because there is too much civilization, too much means of subsistence, too much industry, too much commerce.[17]

To explain this absurdity of capitalism, Marx begins with the "labor theory of value." Just as John Locke (see Chapter 9) had described it, Marx claimed that "products can be measured only by the standard of labour (working time) because they are by nature made from labour."[18]

> Labour is, in the first place, a process in which both man and Nature participate, and in which man of his own accord starts, regulates, and controls the material reactions between himself and Nature. He opposes himself to Nature as one of her own forces, setting in motion arms and legs, head and hands, the natural forces of his body, in order to appropriate Nature's productions in a form adapted to his own wants. By thus acting on the external world and changing it, he at the same time changes his own nature. He develops his slumbering powers and compels them to act in obedience to his sway. We are not now dealing with those primitive instinctive forms of labour that remind us of the mere animals.[19]

The quality that all products share is that they are all products of human labor. Therefore, the difference in value between commodities is the amount of labor invested in them. The difference between a $15 and a $150 pair of shoes is the greater labor put into the latter (care of design, quantity and quality of materials, craftsmanship, etc.). The difference in value between a Ford and a Rolls Royce is the greater labor put into the latter.

Now, in capitalism, labor itself becomes a commodity, to be bought and sold on the market. As John Locke said, 200 years before Marx, with the invention of money (capital) in nondecaying metals and the presence of free labor (people whose only "property" is the strength of their bodies), the worker's production can become the property of his employer, in exchange for wages. But, it is this very arrangement that eventually destroys capitalism through the "crisis of overproduction."[20]

Because labor is a product under capitalism, it can be bought just like any other product. The "price" of labor is the wages paid to hire the worker. The wage level is determined by the market, but as with the cost of other products, it tends towards the cost of "producing" labor (that necessary to maintain the

---

17 Marx, *The Communist Manifesto*, p. 226.
18 Marx, *The Grundrisse* in McLellan, p. 369.
19 Marx, *Capital*, Vol. I, p. 455.
20 Marx, *Capital*, Vol. I, pp. 415–485.

worker). So, workers' wages are set by the labor market at the amount of money needed to keep the working class alive and working.

> The value of labour power is determined, as in the case of every other commodity, by the labour time necessary for the production, and consequently also the reproduction, of this special article. So far as it has value, it represents no more than a definite quantity of the average labour of society incorporated in it. Labour power exists only as a capacity, or power of the living individual. Its production consequently presupposes his existence. Given the individual, the production of labour power consists in his reproduction of himself or his maintenance. For his maintenance he requires a given quantity of the means of subsistence. Therefore the labour time requisite for the production of labour power reduces itself to that necessary for the production of those means of subsistence; in other words, the value of labour power is the value of the means of subsistence necessary for the maintenance of the labourer.[21]

The consequence of this reality is that capitalists can purchase labor-power for less than its "worth" because its "price" (wages) is lower than the value it can create. So, the cost of an hour's labor may be $3.00, but the new value created during that time may be $4.00, and the unpaid excess is taken by the capitalist. Marx calls the value produced by the worker for which he is not paid "surplus value," and this is the source of capitalist *profit*.

> Let us take an example: a tenant farmer gives his day labourer five silver groschen a day. For these five silver groschen the labourer works all day on the farmer's field and thus secures him a return of ten silver groschen. The farmer not only gets the value replaced that he has to give the day labourer, he doubles it. He has therefore employed, consumed, the five silver groschen that he gave to the labourer in a fruitful, productive manner. He has bought with the five silver groschen just that labour and power of the labourer which produces agricultural products of double value and makes ten silver groschen out of five. The day labourer, on the other hand, receives in place of his productive power, the effect of which he has bargained away to the farmer, five silver groschen, and these he consumes with greater or less rapidity. The five silver groschen have, therefore, been consumed in a double way, reproductively for capital, for they have been exchanged for labour power which produced ten silver groschen, unproductively for the worker, for they have been exchanged for means of subsistence which have disappeared forever and the value of which he can only recover by repeating the same exchange with the farmer. Thus capital presupposes wage labour; wage labour presupposes capital. They reciprocally condition the existence of each other; they reciprocally bring forth each other.

---

21 Marx, *Capital*, Vol. I, p. 453.

Does a worker in a cotton factory produce merely cotton textiles? No, he produces capital. He produces values which serve afresh to command his labour and by means of it to create new values.[22]

This is the source of the charge that capitalists "exploit" workers—by "expropriating" a portion of the value they create and not paying for it. Profit is really theft.

But Marx is less concerned with the ethics of the unequal exchange than with its consequences in the capitalist crisis of overproduction.

For Marx argues that the *value* (created by labor) of a product ultimately must equal its *price* on the market (competition forcing prices down to cost of production). In a society in which *workers* are also *consumers*, therefore, the total value of products on the market cannot be completely bought by the workers (who were not paid the full value of their labor). Since capitalists take part of the value in profit and do not spend, but reinvest it, there will always be more supply on the market than demand. This causes the "crisis of overproduction." With too many unbought goods on the market, stores eventually stop placing orders with manufacturers, manufacturers slow down production and lay off workers and, *voila*, a depression, with poverty in the midst of plenty. Such a situation cannot last long before the proletariat overthrows the bourgeoisie, abolishes capitalism in favor of socialism, and, through the *public* ownership of the means of production, eliminates the contradiction between the social forces of production and the private relations of production.

> Hitherto, every form of society has been based, as we have already seen, on the antagonism of oppressing and oppressed classes. But in order to oppress a class, certain conditions must be assured to it under which it can, at least, continue its slavish existence. The serf, in the period of serfdom, raised himself to membership in the commune, just as the petty bourgeois, under the yoke of feudal absolutism, managed to develop into a bourgeois. The modern labourer, on the contrary, instead of rising with the progress of industry, sinks deeper and deeper below the conditions of existence of his own class. He becomes a pauper, and pauperism develops more rapidly than population and wealth. And here it becomes evident, that the bourgeoisie is unfit any longer to be the ruling class in society, and to impose its conditions of existence upon society as an overriding law. It is unfit to rule because it is incompetent to assure an existence to its slave within his slavery, because it cannot help letting him sink into such a state, that it has to feed him, instead of being fed by him. Society can no longer live under this bourgeoisie, in other words, its existence is no longer compatible with society... What the

---

22 Marx, *Wage-Labour and Capital* in McLellan, p. 258.

bourgeoisie, therefore, produces, above all, is its own gravediggers. Its fall and the victory of the proletariat are equally inevitable.[23]

The working class revolution ushers in socialism under the "dictatorship of the proletariat" which leads society into the perfect freedom and peace of a classless communist society. As Marx wrote in a letter to Weydemeyer:

> ...And now as to myself, no credit is due to me for discovering the existence of classes in modern society or the struggle between them. Long before me bourgeois historians had described the historical development of this class struggle and bourgeois economists the economic anatomy of the classes. What I did that was new was to prove: (1) that the existence of classes is only bound up with particular historical phases in the development of production, (2) that the class struggle necessarily leads to the dictatorship of the proletariat, (3) that this dictatorship itself only constitutes the transition to the abolition of all classes and to a classless society....[24]

Social Ethics

The term "*dictatorship* of the proletariat" should not, for Marx, disturb people, since all class societies are dictatorships of some kind, and only the dictatorship of the proletariat leads directly into the human fulfillment of communism. Good social relations, for Marx, are those in which man's nature or "species-being" as a social productive being is realized. Under all class societies, especially capitalism, that is impossible since man is alienated from his truly creative nature. He is oppressed by ruling classes reinforced by ideas of religion, law and politics. Man is ruined by an alienating social system. The one true ethics, for Marx, therefore, are those actions that overthrow the oppressive system and establish the dictatorship of the proletariat. The only moral thing to do is to work for the revolution.

All previous social ethics, for Marx, come from class societies and serve the interests of the ruling, exploiting class. All moral systems, therefore, have served evil. The Thomist appeal to God, Christianity and the hierarchy of laws merely helped the Medieval nobility exploit the peasantry. John Locke's ethics of respecting human rights to Life, Liberty and Property serve the capitalists, who own all the property and steal the worker's labor. So, Marx cares little for "abstract" ethics, which just serve as hypocritical protection of ruling class

---

23 Marx, *The Communist Manifesto*, pp. 230–231.
24 Marx, *The Communist Manifesto*, p. 341.

interest. He reserves his greatest scorn for "bourgeois" ethics of "honesty" and "rights," which serve only to permit capitalists to better plunder the working class. It is not surprising then, that Marxist revolutionaries are happy to discard these outmoded ethics in their struggle to achieve true goodness, freedom and justice through the dictatorship of the proletariat and communism. Such a noble end justifies any means. Violence, deceit, terrorism are all justified by Marxist revolutionaries as necessary and beneficial to the destruction of the evil capitalist system, the ending of hypocritical bourgeois morality and the establishment of perfect peace, freedom and justice in Communism.

As we shall see in the next chapter, Lenin takes this ethic and spreads it worldwide through his analysis of imperialism. Much of international revolution and terrorism is premised in this Marxist-Leninist perspective and justifies violence even against innocent victims.

The Marxist revolutionary ethics are reinforced by his historical perspective that says the revolution is inevitable. History is on the side of the revolutionary saviors of all mankind. Such a glorious view of the mission of Marxists may help to explain the fierce rivalry amongst different revolutionary groups competing to save humanity.

· 14 ·

V.I. LENIN

Imperialism

Vladimir Ilyich Lenin (1870-1924) was a Russian Marxist and leader of the Communist (October) Revolution of 1917 that established the Soviet Union. He headed the U.S.S.R. from 1917 to 1924. Lenin accepted the Marxist principles of human nature, political society and social ethics, but brought them into twentieth century theory through his analysis of Imperialism.

Questions arose about the accuracy of Marxism when, fifty years after the Communist Manifesto, no capitalist country had yet had a socialist revolution. Lenin explained this delay in the workers' revolution with the emergence of capitalist imperialism. Through imperialism, capitalist nations "exported" their economic contradictions to colonial dependencies. In his famous book, *Imperialism, The Highest Stage of Capitalism* (1916), Lenin describes how imperialism helps to preserve the capitalist system, but how it still eventually leads to its own destruction. This analysis of twentieth-century imperialism is widely regarded as a logical extension of Marxist theory and so "Marxism-Leninism" now connotes much of contemporary Communist thought.

Imperialism

Marx had argued in the nineteenth century that the competitive nature of capitalism would lead to fewer and fewer, but larger businesses, as the more efficient capitalists destroyed their rivals in the marketplace. Lenin claimed that by the early twentieth century this concentration of economic power had occurred and that most of the major industries (oil, steel, etc.) had become monopolies.

> Competition becomes transformed into monopoly. The result is immense progress in the socialisation of production. In particular, the process of technical invention and improvement becomes socialised.
>
> This is something quite different from the old free competition between manufacturers, scattered and out of touch with one another, and producing for an unknown market. Concentration has reached the point at which it is possible to make an approximate estimate of all sources of raw materials (for example, the iron ore deposits) of a country and even, as we shall see, of several countries, or of the whole world. Not only are such estimates made, but these sources are captured by gigantic monopolist associations. An approximate estimate of the capacity of markets is also made, and the associations "divide" them up amongst themselves by agreement. Skilled labour is monopolised, the best engineers are engaged; the means of transport are captured-railways in America, ship ping companies in Europe and America. Capitalism in its imperialist stage leads directly to the most comprehensive socialisation of production; it, so to speak, drags the capitalists, against their will and consciousness, into some sort of a new social order, a transitional one from complete free competition to complete socialisation.[1]

This monopoly of economic power in major industries corresponds, for Lenin, to the terrotorial expansion of capitalism to world imperialism. This imperialism, in turn, transforms the class struggle between capitalists and workers into a struggle between imperialist countries (Britain, France, U.S.A., etc.) and the colonial countries (Africa, Asia, Latin America, etc.) they exploit.

> Capitalism has grown into a world system of colonial oppression and of the financial strangulation of the overwhelming majority of the population of the world by a handful of "advanced" countries. And this "booty" is shared between two or three

---

1 V. I. Lenin, Imperialism, *The Highest Stage of Capitalism*, in V. I. Lenin, *Selected Works*, Vol. I. (Moscow, Progress Publishers, 1970), p. 686.

powerful world plunderers armed to the teeth (America, Great Britain, Japan), who are drawing the world into *their* war over the division of *their* booty.[2]

According to Lenin, the world of 1900 had been divided up by the imperialist countries, as each capitalist nation strove to control more of what today we would call the "Third World."

> We clearly see from these figures how "complete" was the partition of the world at the turn of the twentieth century. After 1876 colonial possessions increased to enormous dimensions, by more than fifty per cent, from 40,000,000 to 65,000,000 square kilometres for the six biggest powers; the increase amounts to 25,000,000 square kilometres, fifty percent more than the area of the metropolitan countries (16,500,000 square kilometres). In 1876 three powers had no colonies, and a fourth, France, had scarcely any. By 1914 these four powers had acquired colonies with an area of 14,100,000 square kilometres, i.e., about half as much again as the area of Europe, with a population of nearly 100,000,000.[3]

The driving force behind such capitalist imperialism, for Lenin, was the inherent contradiction in capitalism and the periodic crises of overproduction that threatened a proletarian revolution. Imperialism provided raw materials, new markets for excess goods and cheap labor. Labor was so cheap in the impoverished colonies, that capitalists could make "superprofits" there and use them to "bribe" their native working class into submission.[4] Thus imperialism allowed capital to further exploit human labor abroad while turning their domestic working class into a "labor aristocracy," with high union wages, benefits, etc.

> Obviously, out of such enormous *superprofits* (since they are obtained over and above the profits which capitalists squeeze out of the workers of their "own" country) it is *possible to bribe* the labour leaders and the upper stratum of the labour aristocracy. And that is just what the capitalists of the "advanced" countries are doing: they are bribing them in a thousand different ways, direct and indirect, overt and covert.[5]

These higher paid workers in the imperialist country are thus "bought off" and, for Lenin, become "bourgeoisified."

---

2 Lenin, p. 674.
3 Lenin, p. 730.
4 Lenin, p. 677.
5 Lenin, p. 677.

And in speaking of the British working class the bourgeois student of "British imperialism at the beginning of the twentieth century" is obliged to distinguish systematically between the *"upper stratum"* of the workers and the *"lower stratum of the proletariat proper"*. The upper stratum furnishes the bulk of the membership of co-operatives, of trade unions, of sporting clubs and of numerous religious sects. To this level is adapted the electoral system, which in Great Britain is still *"sufficiently restricted to exclude the lower stratum of the proletariat proper"*! In order to present the condition of the British working class in a rosy light, only this upper stratum—which constitutes a *minority* of the proletariat—is usually spoken of.[6]

This stratum of workers-turned-bourgeois, or the labour aristocracy, who are quite philistine in their mode of life, in the size of their earnings and in their entire outlook, is the principal prop of the Second International, and in our days, the principal *social* (not military) *prop of the bourgeoisie.* For they are *the real agents of the bourgeoisie in the workingclass* movement, the labour lieutenants of the capitalist class, real vehicles of reformism and chauvinism. In the civil war between the proletariat and the bourgeoisie they inevitably, and in no small numbers, take the side of the bourgeoisie, the "Versaillese" against the "Communards."[7]

So, imperialism, through which the advanced industrial countries exploit the underdeveloped colonies, provides both high profits and domestic peace for the capitalists. But, Lenin asserts, the desperate search for new colonies by all capitalist countries eventually causes fierce rivalries amongst competing imperialist nations and world wars.[8]

As the exploitation of colonies and imperialistic wars become more and more terrible, revolutions, or wars of "national liberation," will take place in the colonies, expelling the capitalists and establishing socialism. Thus, proletarian revolutions will occur in the "underdeveloped" nations (such as Russia, China and Latin America) first, rather than in the advanced capitalist countries, as Marx had predicted. But, asserts Lenin, as more colonies have socialist revolutions, the contradictions and crises of capitalism will return to haunt the host country, eventually causing working-class revolution there also.

In the meantime, the imperialist countries have become fat and lazy, living off the "superprofits" of colonial labor, exporting more and more manufacturing to Third World countries, and becoming, thereby, "parasitic." As the imperialist nations, increasingly working only in "service" industries and banking, loose their colonies, their privation will be all the more sudden, prompting a

---

6 Lenin, p. 750.
7 Lenin, p. 677.
8 Lenin, p. 672, 674, 748.

quick socialist revolution at home. Contemporary Marxist-Leninists see the revolutions in Africa and Latin America as defeating capitalist imperialism and bringing the revolution inevitably back to the United States.

> For that reason the term "rentier state" (Rentnerstaat), or usurer state, is coming into common use in the economic literature that deals with imperialism. The world has become divided into a handful of usurer states and a vast majority of debtor states. "At the top of the list of foreign investments," says Schulze-Gaevernitz, "are those placed in politically dependent or allied countries: Great Britain grants loans to Egypt, Japan, China and South America. Her navy plays here the part of bailiff in case of necessity. Great Britain's political power protects her from the indignation of her debtors." Sartorius von Waltershausen in his book, *The National Economic System of Capital Investments Abroad*, cites Holland as the model "rentier state" and points out that Great Britain and France are now becoming such. Schilder is of the opinion that five industrial states have become "definitely pronounced creditor countries": Great Britain, France, Germany, Belgium and Switzerland. He does not include Holland in this list simply because she is "industrially little developed." The United States is a creditor only of the American countries....[9]
>
> The rentier state is a state of parasitic, decaying capitalism, and this circumstance cannot fail to influence all the socio political conditions of the countries concerned, in general, and the two fundamental trends in the working-class movement, in particular.[10]

Marxism-Leninism informs many of the Third World revolutionary movements of our time. The Russian, Chinese, Vietnamese and Nicaraguan revolutions were all fought under the banners of "expel the imperialists," "down with capitalist-imperialist exploitation," etc. Today's radical movements in Africa and Latin America decry "neocolonial oppression" and "imperialistic exploitation." They interpret America's support for military dictatorships as evidence of their reactionary, imperialistic plan to oppress colonial dependencies and plunder the Third World. Even a movement in the Roman Catholic Church in Latin America ("Liberation Theology") employs Marxist-Leninist analysis to explain Third World poverty and struggle for revolution. Liberation theologians claim that Christ called us to help the poor, that Marxist philosophy shows us how to best do that, and that socialism approaches the Kingdom of God.[11] The Vatican has reproached such casual mixing of Marxism and Christianity, but the appeal

---

9 Lenin, p. 746.
10 Lenin, p. 747.
11 See Gustavo Gutierrez, *A Theory of Liberation* (New York, 1977).

of Liberation Theology in Latin America reveals the continuing presence of Lenin's analysis of imperialism.

· 15 ·

SIGMUND FREUD

Psychology and Society

Sigmund Freud (1856-1939) was an Austrian medical psychologist and the founder of psychoanalysis. Born in Freiberg, Moravia (what is now Czechoslovakia), Freud was educated in Vienna and Paris. His interest in psychological therapy began with his treatment of hysteria with hypnosis. His discovery that unpleasant memories can be repressed into the unconscious mind, affecting conscious behavior, but brought out through hypnosis or word association formed the basis of psychoanalysis and psychotherapy. Not content with the merely therapeutic applications of this discovery, Freud constructed an elaborate and highly pessimistic theory of man's anthropological origins and place in nature and society. His emphasis on the irrational (and destructive) impulses in man is in sharp contrast to both liberal and Marxist notions of man's goodness and social progress.

Human Nature

Freud distinguished three elements in man's psychology: the Id, the Ego and the Super-Ego. The Id is man's primitive impulses, especially sexual impulses, which use others as objects and destroy anyone who interferes with the satisfaction of their desire. The Ego is man's rational capacity, which allows him to act effectively in the everyday world. The Super-Ego is a distillate of the pressures and requirements of family and society (represented in the authority of the father, the State and the moral precepts of the Church).

> The ego represents what we call reason and sanity, in contrast to the id which contains the passions....
>
> The functional importance of the ego is manifested in the fact that normally control over the approaches to motility devolves upon it. Thus in its relation to the id it is like a man on horseback, who has to hold in check the superior strength of the horse; with this difference, that the rider seeks to do so with his own strength while the ego uses borrowed forces....[1]
>
> For that which prompted the person to form an ego-ideal, over which his conscience keeps guard, was the influence of parental criticism (conveyed to him by the medium of the voice), reinforced, as time went on, by those who trained and taught the child and by all the other persons of his environment—an indefinite host, too numerous to reckon (fellow-men, public opinion).[2]

The Ego and Super-Ego are necessary to keep the Id sufficiently in check to allow the individual to function in society, but when they excessively repress the libido (sexual drives)—which for Freud they invariably do to some extent—the individual can become neurotic and obsessive. Psychoanalysis can help uncover the repressed desire and help the Ego deal with it. However, Freud sees inevitable tension and conflict in man's nature and between man's instincts and social harmony. Human Nature for Freud, after Hobbes, is fundamentally materialistic and dominated by aggressive following of physical drives.

> The element of truth behind all this, which people are so ready to disavow, is that men are not gentle creatures who want to be loved, and who at the most can defend themselves if they are attacked; they are, on the contrary, creatures among whose instinctual endowments is to be reckoned a powerful share of aggressiveness. As a result, their neighbour is for them not only a potential helper or sexual object, but also someone who tempts them to satisfy their aggressiveness on him, to exploit his capacity for work without compensation, to use him sexually without his consent, to seize his possessions, to humiliate him, to cause him pain, to torture and to kill

---

1   Sigmund Freud, *The Ego and the Id* in *A General Selection from the Works of Sigmund Freud*, edited by John Rickman (New York, Anchor: Doubleday, 1957), p. 215.
2   Freud, *On Narcissism* in *A General Selection...*, p. 118.

him. *Homo homini lupus.* Who, in the face of all his experience of life and of history, will have the courage to dispute this assertion? As a rule this cruel aggressiveness waits for some provocation or puts itself at the service of some other purpose, whose goal might also have been reached by milder measures. In circumstances that are favourable to it, when the mental counterforces which ordinarily inhibit it are out of action, it also manifests itself spontaneously and reveals man as a savage beast to whom consideration towards his own kind is something alien. Anyone who calls to mind the atrocities committed during the racial migrations or the invasions of the Huns, or by the people known as Mongols under Jenghiz Khan and Tamerlane, or at the capture of Jerusalem by the pious Crusaders, or even, indeed, the horrors of the recent World War—anyone who calls these things to mind will have to bow humbly before the truth of this view.[3]

Men are motivated by pleasure and pain, and the pursuit of these private impulses invariably leads to conflict with others and the world.

We will therefore turn to the less ambitious question of what men themselves show by their behavior to be the purpose and intention of their lives. What do they demand of life and wish to achieve in it? The answer to this can hardly be in doubt. They strive after happiness; they want to become happy and to remain so. This endeavour has two sides, a positive and a negative aim. It aims, on the one hand, at an absence of pain and unpleasure, and, on the other, at the experiencing of strong feelings of pleasure. In its narrower sense the word 'happiness' only relates to the last. In conformity with this dichotomy in his aims, man's activity develops in two directions, according as it seeks to realize—in the main, or even exclusively—the one or the other of these aims.

As we see, what decides the purpose of life is simply the programme of the pleasure principle. This principle dominates the operation of the mental apparatus from the start. There can be no doubt about its efficacy, and yet its programme is at loggerheads with the whole world, with the macrocosm as much as with the microcosm. There is no possibility at all of its being carried through; all the regulations of the universe run counter to it. One feels inclined to say that the intention that man should be 'happy' is not included in the plan of 'Creation.'[4]

Thus, for Freud, man cannot be happy, even though he attempts to be through various diversions.

---

3   Sigmund Freud, *Civilization and Its Discontents*, translated by James Strachey (New York, W.W. Norton, 1961).
4   Freud, *Civilization and Its Discontents*, p. 23.

> Life, as we find it, is too hard for us; it brings us too many pains, disappointments and impossible tasks. In order to bear it we cannot dispense with palliative measures. 'We cannot do without auxiliary constructions', as Theodor Fontane tells us. There are perhaps three such measures: powerful deflections, which cause us to make light of our misery; substitutive satisfactions, which diminish it; and intoxicating substances, which make us insensitive to it.[5]

All of these attempts at human happiness are doomed to failure, even drinking and work.

> For one knows that, with the help of this 'drowner of cares' one can at any time withdraw from the pressure of reality and find refuge in a world of one's own with better conditions of sensibility. As is well known, it is precisely this property of intoxicants which also determines their danger and their injuriousness. They are responsible, in certain circumstances, for the useless waste of a large quota of energy which might have been employed for the improvement of the human lot.[6]

> It is not possible, within the limits of a short survey, to discuss adequately the significance of work for the economics of the libido. No other technique for the conduct of life attaches the individual so firmly to reality as laying emphasis on work; for his work at least gives him a secure place in a portion of reality, in the human community. The possibility it offers of displacing a large amount of libidinal components, whether narcissistic, aggressive or even erotic, on to professional work and on to the human relations connected with it lends it a value by no means second to what it enjoys as something indispensible to the preservation and justification of existence in society. Professional activity is a source of special satisfaction if it is a freely chosen one—if, that is to say, by means of sublimation, it makes possible the use of existing inclinations, of persisting or constitutionally reinforced instinctual impulses. And yet, as a path to happiness, work is not highly prized by men. They do not strive after it as they do after other possibilities of satisfaction. The great majority of people only work under the stress of necessity, and this natural human aversion to work raises most difficult social problems.[7]

Freud is particularly scornful of attempts to identify intellectual effort as a substitute for libidinal impulses; he would hardly agree with John Stuart Mill's adherence to these "higher" activities.

---

5   Freud, *Civilization and Its Discontents*, p. 22.
6   Freud, *Civilization and Its Discontents*, p. 25.
7   Freud, *Civilization and Its Discontents*, p. 27.

At present we can only say figuratively that such satisfactions seem 'finer and higher'. But their intensity is mild as compared with that derived from the sating of crude and primary instinctual impulses; it does not convulse our physical being. And the weak point of this method is that it is not applicable generally: it is accessible to only a few people. It presupposes the possession of special dispositions and gifts which are far from being common to any practical degree. And even to the few who do possess them, this method cannot give complete protection from suffering. It creates no impenetrable armour against the arrows of fortune, and it habitually fails when the source of suffering is a person's own body.[8]

Spiritual feelings hold no interest for Freud, who regards all religion as an infantile illusion of the Super-Ego projecting the father's authority and power onto cosmic proportions.[9] Man's nature is dominated by physical impulses: hunger and sex.

...I took as my starting-point a saying of the poet-philosopher, Schiller, that 'hunger and love are what moves the world'. Hunger could be taken to represent the instincts which aim at preserving the individual; while love strives after objects, and its chief function, favoured in every way by nature, is the preservation of the species. Thus, to begin with, ego-instincts and object-instincts confronted each other. It was to denote the energy of the latter and only the latter instincts that I introduced the term 'libido'. Thus the antithesis was between the ego-instincts and the 'libidinal' instincts of love (in its widest sense) which were directed to an object.[10]

Erotic impulses do drive man into society, if only to satisfy his lust,[11] but once there, they lead to his frustration, as social rules restrict the satisfaction of his desires.

In the developmental process of the individual, the programme of the pleasure principle, which consists in finding the satisfaction of happiness, is retained as the main aim. Integration in, or adaptation to, a human community appears as a scarcely avoidable condition which must be fulfilled before this aim of happiness can be achieved. If it could be done without that condition, it would perhaps be preferable. To put it in other words, the development of the individual seems to us to be a product of the interaction between two urges, the urge towards happiness, which we usually call 'egoistic', and the urge towards union with others in

---

8   Freud, *Civilization and Its Discontents*, pp. 26-27.
9   See Sigmund Freud, *The Future of an Illusion*, translated by John Rickman (New York, 1961).
10 Freud, *Civilization and Its Discontents*, p. 64.
11 Freud, *Civilization and Its Discontents*, p. 69.

> the community, which we call 'altruistic'. Neither of these descriptions goes much below the surface. In the process of individual development, as we have said, the main accent falls mostly on the egoistic urge (or the urge towards happiness); while the other urge, which may be described as a 'cultural' one, is usually content with the role of imposing restrictions.[12]
>
> If civilization imposes such great sacrifices not only on man's sexuality but on his aggressivity, we can understand better why it is hard for him to be happy in that civilization. In fact, primitive man was better off in knowing no restrictions of instinct. To counterbalance this, his prospects of enjoying this happiness for any length of time were very slender. Civilized man has exchanged a portion of his possibilities of happiness for a portion of security.[13]

Political Society

All states, for Freud, develop to coordinate individuals' work together, but in the process, inhibit and frustrate his natural impulses. Freud describes in anthropological terms the origins of civilization.

> After primal man had discovered that it lay in his owns hands, literally, to improve his lot on earth by working, it cannot have been a matter of indifference to him whether another man worked with or against him. The other man acquired the value for him of a fellow-worker, with whom it was useful to live together. Even earlier, in his ape-like prehistory, man had adopted the habit of forming families, and the members of his family were probably his first helpers. One may suppose that the founding of families was connected with the fact that a moment came when the need for genital satisfaction no longer made its appearance like a guest who drops in suddenly, and, after his departure, is heard of no more for a long time, but instead took up its quarters as a permanent lodger. When this happened, the male acquired a motive for keeping the female, or, speaking more generally, his sexual objects, near him; while the female, who did not want to be separated from her helpless young, was obliged, in their interests, to remain with the stronger male.[14]

Politics is simply the rule of the strongest over the weakness or the majority over the minority, but all restrict the individual's natural liberty.

---

12 Freud, *Civilization and Its Discontents*, p. 87.
13 Freud, *Civilization and Its Discontents*, p. 62.
14 Freud, *Civilization and Its Discontents*, p. 46.

> Human life in common is only made possible when a majority comes together which is stronger than any separate individual and which remains united against all separate individuals. The power of this community is then set up as 'right' in opposition to the power of the individual, which is condemned as 'brute force'. This replacement of the power of the individual by the power of a community constitutes the decisive step of civilization. The essence of it lies in the fact that the members of the community restrict themselves in their possibilities of satisfaction, whereas the individuals knew no such restrictions.[15]

> The liberty of the individual is no gift of civilization. It was greatest before there was any civilization, though then, it is true, it had for the most part no value, since the individual was scarcely in a position to defend it. The development of civilization imposes restrictions on it, and justice demands that no one shall escape those restrictions. What makes itself felt in a human community as a desire for freedom may be their revolt against some existing injustice, and so may prove favourable to a further development of civilization; it may remain compatible with civilization. But it may also spring from the remains of their original personality, which is still untamed by civilization and may thus become the basis in them of hostility to civilization. The urge for freedom, therefore, is directed against particular forms and demands of civilization or against civilization altogether.[16]

Thus, civilization forces the repression and sublimation of man's instincts. The libidinal energy is transferred into economic, scientific and artistic activities, to the benefit of culture; but man's sexual urges remain frustrated.

> Sublimation of instinct is an especially conspicuous feature of cultural development; it is what makes it possible for higher psychical activities, scientific, artistic or ideological, to play such an important part in civilized life. If one were to yield to a first impression, one would say that sublimation is a vicissitude which has been forced upon the instincts entirely by civilization. But it would be wiser to reflect upon this a little longer. In the third place, finally, and this seems the most important of all, it is impossible to overlook the extent to which civilization is built up upon a renunciation of instinct, how much it presupposes precisely the non-satisfaction (by suppression, repression or some other means?) of powerful instincts. This 'cultural frustration' dominates the large field of social relationships between human beings.[17]

This is the source of man's misery and mental illness.

---

15 Freud, *Civilization and Its Discontents*, p. 42.
16 Freud, *Civilization and Its Discontents*, pp. 42–43.
17 Freud, *Civilization and Its Discontents*, p. 44.

> This contention holds that what we call our civilization is largely responsible for our misery, and that we should be much happier if we gave it up and returned to primitive conditions a person becomes neurotic because he cannot tolerate the amount of frustration which society imposes on him in the service of its cultural ideals, and it was inferred from this that the abolition or reduction of those demands would result in a return to possibilities of happiness.[18]

Social Ethics

Freud dismisses ethical and religious values as expressions of the SuperEgo which civilization uses to control human impulses and which leads to frustration and neurosis.

> Ethics is thus to be regarded as a therapeutic attempt-as an endeavour to achieve, by means of a command of the super-ego, something which has so far not been achieved by means of any other cultural activities. As we already know, the problem before us is how to get rid of the greatest hindrance to civilization-namely, the constitutional inclination of human beings to be aggressive towards one another....[19]

His own conception of the "good" individual would probably be one whose Ego balanced the impulses of the Id with the restrictions of the Super-Ego. He suggests that this may best be accomplished by a variety of pleasurable activities.

> Just as a cautious business-man avoids tying up all his capital in one concern, so, perhaps, worldly wisdom will advise us not to look for the whole of our satisfaction from a single aspiration. Its success is never certain, for that depends on the convergence of many factors, perhaps on none more than on the capacity of the psychical constitution to adapt its function to the environment and then to exploit that environment for a yield of pleasure.[20]

A good society might be one that is not so restrictive of libidinal impulses that it breeds mass neurosis, but is sufficiently strict to control man's worse excesses.

Freud's ideas spawned twentieth century psychoanalysis and psychotherapy, though soon other theories modified his emphasis on aggression and sex, especially those of Carl Jung and Alfred Adler.

---

18 Freud, *Civilization and Its Discontents*, pp. 33-34.
19 Freud, *Civilization and Its Discontents*, p. 89.
20 Freud, *Civilization and Its Discontents*, p. 31.

· 16 ·

GIOVANNI GENTILE

Fascism

Giovanni Gentile (1875-1944) is considered the philosopher of Italian Fascism. He was born in Sicily, educated at Pisa and served as Professor of Philosophy at the universities of Palermo, Pisa and Rome. His writings range from studies of Marx and Hegel to essays on art, education and politics. His political theory is found in the book, *Genesis and Structure of Society*. With Mussolini's rise to power in 1922, Gentile became Minister of Public Instruction and was able to implement many of his ideas for educational reform. In 1925, Gentile became President of the National Fascist Institute of Culture and Director of the *Encyclopedia italiana* (the definitive representation of the Fascist worldview). In 1944, after Mussolini's fall from power, Gentile was assassinated by a group of Italian Communists.

Gentile's Fascist theory is influenced by Hegel's philosophy of the Dialectic. Hegel's Dialectic posits that reality consists of the unity of opposites in a single whole and that truth is knowledge of that unity with diversity. Marx was originally a "Left Hegelian," with the Dialectic seen as expressed in class struggle. Fascism also employs Hegelian Dialectics, but with very different results.

Human Nature

Gentile conceived of human nature in a dialectical sense as consisting of the opposites of the "particular" individual with the "universal" person. One's particularity resides in the separate nature of the body and the private desires and interests resulting from it. The universal quality of the individual comes from the "community" that is within him. That community includes both the present community of nation and the past community of race and blood. Thus, man's social nature derives from his identity in a nation and a heritage in race. These, for Gentile, do not obviate the individual's distinctive personality; rather, they give it identity and reality. In this dialectical view, the individual knows himself by being consciously aware of his relations in the world with his race, heritage, nationality, family and class. So, for Fascism, the more one realizes oneself in the "otherness" of race and blood, the more one actually develops his individuality.

> The people have two 'voices.' There is one that is only the *ratio cognoscendi* of truth and of all value-a sign but not an argument. This is the Ciceronian *consensus gentium*. But there is another that is rather the *ratio essendi* of the truth, and this is the one that matters, the only one that can serve as the norm for a man's conduct: the voice of an ideal people immanent within him, which speaks to him without leave, without delay, and without hesitation, giving him courage to live, to speak, and to act, and sustaining him from within as the source of his own strength—the voice of the ideal Church that every believer has within him, completely at one with his own soul....The Italian who feels that he is an Italian speaks for all Italy; and the man for mankind; the father for all fathers, the son for all sons, the soldier for all soldiers, and so on-each for all....the existence of an ideal community within the individual does not abolish his individuality or his absolute independence of tradition, and of everything—customs, institutions, or what you will—that may appear to be the actually existent form of the community. Let us take language as our example again, for in this field the life of the spirit has been most carefully explored. It is obvious that every writer completely renews his linguistic material, molding it through the originality of his style into a shape of his own; and not strictly abiding by the usage of the ancients, as the purists do, nor yet by that of the so-called living language employed by the modernists—a usage already defined in the dictionaries and rule books that contain the linguistic patrimony of a nation. And what happens with language happens with everything else that enters into the life of the spirit. There is no imitation or repetition and nothing is preserved intact; everything is renewed. The man who lives a truly human life is bound to be an innovator, a creator who lets nothing leave his forge, as it were, that does not bear the stamp of his own personality.

> But when we say that every "I" is really "We," and that an ideal community is present and active in every individual, we do not mean that there is a plurality of persons already in existence prior to the act of the individual, or that the community is a legacy from the past....To sum up then: in the individual, particularity and universality coincide. The more he is himself the more closely he is identified with all men.[1]

So, man's nature is dialectical, contradictory, and the separate individual must participate in the community "outside" himself to truly know the social nature that is within him.

> The human individual is not an atom. Immanent in the concept of an individual is the concept of society. For there is no ego, no real individual, who does not have within him (rather than just with him) an *alter* who is his essential *socius*—that is to say, an object that is not a mere 'thing' opposed to him as subject, but a subject like himself.[2]

> As long as the individual has not dissolved and ideally destroyed his own particularity through the power of this inner universality—and strictly speaking he has always destroyed it and yet never succeeds in destroying it—he has not yet found himself, he is not a true individual....In this dialectic of individuality the immanence of community in the individual becomes manifest; for he cannot set his feet on the solid earth of the particular without raising his head in the free air of universality and establishing himself in the world of liberty.[3]

The dialectic of human nature produces a particular will representing one's solitary, private interest, and a universal will, representing one's community interest. For Gentile, the only way to reconcile these conflicting wills is by participating in the Fascist State, whose laws contain the sum of all universal wills.

> A nation is not to be defined in terms of common soil or common life, and the consequent community of traditions and customs, language or religion, etc. All this is only the matter of the nation, not its form; for the nation can only exist where men are conscious of this matter, and accept it in their hearts as the substantial content of the national personality and the proper object of the national will, the will which gains concrete and actual expression in the State.[4]

---

1   Giovanni Gentile, *Genesis and Structure of Society*, translated by H. S. Harris (Urbana, University of Illinois Press, 1966), pp. 84-85.
2   Gentile, p. 98.
3   Gentile, p. 89.
4   Gentile, p. 121.

Fascism, then, denies the strict separation of individual and State. If the individual is conscious of his universal will, he will be unified with the State as part of his nature. The powerful Fascist State, therefore, is not opposed to the rights of citizens, but rather is necessary for their realization.

> This same positivity reappears in the opposition between government and governed, which is wrongly but generally confused with the duality of State and citizens. The government (whether absolute or representative) makes the law and sees to its observance; and those subject to it must take its activity for granted if they are to be governed. And in the abstract that is how it is. But just as positive law is canceled in actual ethical action, so all opposition between government and governed vanishes in the consent of the latter, without which the government cannot stand.

> This consent may be spontaneous or it may be procured by coercion. The moral ideal of the State, within which the government exercises its authority, requires that spontaneity be increased to a maximum and coercion reduced to a minimum; but it is impossible that either element should ever stand alone, unaccompanied by its opposite. The nations swing restlessly between the two poles of a minimum of coercion with a maximum of spontaneity: between democracy and absolutism, for it is very hard to attain that mutual tempering of the opposed principles which is their dialectical synthesis.[5]

So, the political state is natural for human beings, as their universal wills find expression in it, and they know themselves consciously through it.

Political Society

The Fascist State, for Gentile, represents the universal wills of all its citizens through law.

> The will of the State is *law*—'public' or 'private' law, accordingly as it regulates the relations between the State and the citizen, or between one citizen and another. In any case the will of the State is actually expressed in the will of the citizen so far as the citizen's will possesses universal validity. There is no such thing as right or law apart from the State, and any individual who 'asserts his rights' must always appeal to a universal will to which all private inclinations must submit just because they are only inclinations.

---

5   Gentile, pp. 123–124.

> But are we speaking here of *positive law*? Law is not worth anything unless it is positive, for only positive law has the effective authority of universal will over private inclination.[6]

Law embodies the universal will and common heritage of the people and rises above particular economic or social interests. Fascism criticizes both liberal democracy and communism for denying this universal quality of law. In liberal democracies, Gentile argues, law is simply the interest of the most powerful group or class. In Communist societies, law expresses the interest of one class- the working class. Only Fascist law reflects the common good of the universal will, respecting the diversity of particular wills in society, but not allowing them to dominate public life.

> The problem of the State today is no longer to secure the political recognition of the third estate—which was the task of liberalism—but to secure for the worker and his syndicates the political significance which they claim but which they can never possess until the pluralism of the syndicates is reconciled in the unity of the State. For man considered as a political animal is the State; and he is one State, or he is nothing. Whereas the syndicates, being groups of individuals arranged according to the economic categories of production in which they are employed, are like a crowd of individuals, each different from all the rest and therefore solitary, not disposed to recognize any but his own private interest. So the State is not a syndicate, but the reconciliation and resolution of the syndicates in the fundamental unity of humanity which is articulated in and through all of the syndical categories; and this unity is not a result, but rather the basic principle that makes the pluralism of the syndicates possible.[7]

In such State unity, there is no conflict between authority and liberty, as both reside in the individual and are reconciled in the State. Gentile argues that only in liberal democracies which, after Locke, conceive of individuals as separate atoms, is the conflict between State authority and personal liberty a problem.

> There is much talk nowadays of authoritarian governments and liberal governments, which is all based on the abstract opposition of authority and liberty, the government and the individuals governed. The individuals are conceived as atoms, each one standing on his own and possessing in himself all the rights and duties that have any meaning for him; and the government is thought of as a purely limiting power which coordinates the free activities of the individuals. People are

---

6   Gentile, p. 122.
7   Gentile, pp. 128–129.

unwilling to recognize that the choice of suitable machinery for the tempering of the two opposed principles is not a problem to be solved by reference to eternal principles, but in accordance with historical criteria founded on considerations of expediency appropriate to different historical situations. These are matters of degree in which the intuition of a statesman is worth more than the theorems of a political scientist.

What the philosopher ought always to emphasize is that authority must not destroy liberty, nor should liberty pretend to do without authority. For neither of the two terms can stand alone; and the necessity of their synthesis is a consequence of the essentially dialectical character of the spiritual act.[8]

The universal will of the State is superior to particular economic or class interests; neither labor nor capital should dictate politics for the whole nation.

The State is concrete universal will, whereas economics is concerned with the sub-human life of man-the corporeal, natural, subhuman element that has its place in human consciousness, but only as an abstract moment already transcended.

It follows that there is an economic element in the will, and hence in the State; but it has been transcended, transfigured by the light of freedom, and endowed with ethical and spiritual value....

The claim of pure economics to interfere in politics and to dictate laws to the State without taking into account the special historical problems that arise in the total context of actual social life is a perpetual source of irreconcilable conflicts between the theoretical economists, secure in the mathematical stronghold that keeps them safe from any unpleasant encounter with reality, and the politicians, who are all too conscious of the heavy burden of their responsibility to society.[9]

However, because no single economic class or group can control the State in Fascism, the private market economy is permitted to exist (albeit regulated for the common good), because the Marxist alternative (the "dictatorship of the proletariat") represents a particular class will. Therefore, Marxists have always regarded Fascism as an especially violent dictatorship of the bourgeoisie, protecting capitalism from the revolutionary working class under the guise of the "universal will." Fascists in both Italy and Germany persecuted Marxists.

---

8   Gentile, pp. 124-125.
9   Gentile, pp. 147-148.

Liberal democracies (such as Britain and the United States) have traditionally regarded both Fascism and Communism as "authoritarian," because both deny that government should be limited to protecting private rights. Gentile regards this "bourgeois" concern with private rights as one-sided and denying man's "universal" social character.

Similarly, Fascism's approach to religion and politics is distinct from both Communism and liberalism. While Communist states suppress religion as a tool of class oppression and liberalism establishes the separation of church and state and total freedom of religion, Fascism insists that religion is essential to the individual and the state as moral entities. The just state for Gentile must neither be hostile nor indifferent towards religion.

> There is no State that does not concern itself in one way or another, positively or negatively, with religion, oscillating between theocracy and a State religion on the one hand, and complete separation of Church and State in an agnostic pseudo-liberal democracy on the other. Even this latter attitude is polemical in a way that is inconsistent with its pretended agnosticism. No State can ignore the religion of its people, any more than it can be indifferent about their customs, or their moral attitudes, or anything else so closely connected with their political life. The reason for this necessary connection between the State and religion must be sought in the very nature of the former. The purpose of the State is to achieve peace, and the rule of law which is its outward manifestation; or in other words, it seeks to achieve unity in the popular consciousness because of its immanent tendency to realize the will of the people. But the will of the people is the universal will of man; and the universal will of man is religion, or more precisely it contains religion. The will is self-concept; and as such it is religion both in the moment of subjective immediacy (the divine spark that we all feel within us) and again in the moment of objective immediacy (when reality seems complete and leaves no place for man, who therefore bows the knee before it and adores it).
>
> So that the State could not be the fulfillment of man's humanity if it did not contain religion. A completely secular consciousness, or a completely secular State, is a figment of the imagination.[10]

Of course, the Fascist governments in both Italy and Germany expected the support of the Church, and those clergy who criticized or resisted them in the name of Christ (such as Dietrich Bonhoeffer) were often persecuted, as violating the "universal will."

---

10 Gentile, pp. 149–150.

International Relations

Gentile applies the Fascist dialectic to relations between states. Given the aggressive behavior of Fascist states in this century, it is interesting to see how Gentile justifies war as part of the dialectic. War arises out of the inevitable tension between different nations. But when the Fascist State invades and conquers a neighboring country, it creates a new "unity" among opposites.

> The moment of *otherness* is essential as the moment of pure objectivity in the dynamism of self-consciousness. The other ness is destined to be transcended; but it has to be there, and it has to be conquered. First there must be the opposition, and then the conciliation and the unity. This is the eternal rhythm of human social life, the rhythm of moral development. Master and pupil, parent and child, teacher and learner, lord and slave, dominant peoples and dominated peoples (where superior civilization may be the index of superior power or vice versa), these are all original and inevitable oppositions which spiritual activity transcends and reconciles. And among the methods of transcending opposition is war. The philosopher must recognize that there are a thousand forms of war and that these forms are multiplying with the multiplication of the ways in which human thought is expressed, and the human will made effective. There is war with pin pricks and war with cannon balls. The pin pricks are only words; but the words are used in pursuit of aims substantially similar to those for which cannon balls are employed-the annihilation of the enemy. War; properly so-called, however, is conflict between States waged with all the most murderous weapons, in order to establish their rights when one of them hinders another in the attaining of ends that are essential to its existence; and the resolution of the struggle does not really consist in the annihilation of one of the contestants, but in the destruction of that antagonism of the will which is what sustains the contest. The enemy must be placed in a position in which he can no more offend; and he must recognize our will as his own. He must therefore survive to set the seal on our victory by his recognition.
>
> Thus war does not derive from an inhuman desire for solitude. The other people, with whom we disagree, are our collaborators; they play their part in the formation of that spiritual organization or patrimony which is our world. The cause of war is only dissent, and its end therefore is nothing but the conquest of this dissent.[11]

---

11 Gentile, pp. 164–165.

The Family

Fascism places special emphasis on the role of the family in developing the individual's universal consciousness. The family draws the person "outside" himself and nurtures the identity with others. This prepares the individual for participation in the larger "others" of race, society and nation.

> But man cannot be weighed as an atom as he is in communist theory. Man is the family. An individual labors for himself but also for his children: "he plants trees for another generation." The State has an interest in cultivating and developing the instinct (which in man becomes a vocation) toward the procreation and recognition of offspring; and hence it has an interest in the formation of the family nucleus through which the individual is led to natural impulses to break the crust of his selfish egoism and ignore the boundaries of his natural individuality.[12]

Social Ethics

Fascist theory identifies goodness, both individual and social, with conscious realization of self as dialectically universal and particular. The moral person knows his nature as both individual and community and the just State knows itself as the universal will of particular beings. In both cases, goodness resides in a kind of knowledge or self-realization.

> In concrete experience the political activity of man is identical with ethical activity since the will resolves the otherness of society ad infinitum, and thus absorbs the whole world of social relations into the infinite process of its self-realization.[13]

Thus, the bourgeois individual in a liberal democracy that acknowledges only separate identity and private interest is incomplete and the Marxist in a Communist State that represents only the productive side of man and the proletarian interest is narrow and oppressive. Only the Fascist State, for Gentile, represents the total person and justly reconciles his contradictory natures, universal and particular, in the oneness of the State.

> In any case, the distinction can no longer be maintained when the empirical character of all distinctions between 'individual' and 'society' or 'individual' and 'State' is recognized; for, as we have seen, the State exists already in the private individual,

---

12 Gentile, p. 172.
13 Gentile, p. 175.

and every empirical State is only a development of a new form of this original transcendental State. What is vital is that we should attribute to the transcendental State the absolute infinite universality that belongs to it from the beginning; then the imagination will not compel us to break open this infinity and conceive a wider State, which can never be anything but an empty fancy. For at any given time the only State that really exists is the one that expresses our own perpetually infinite and absolutely universal will.[14]

Of the three dominant political theories of the twentieth century (liberalism, Communist and Fascism), Fascism was both the most aggressive and the most short-lived. Both liberal democracy and Marxist Communism condemn Fascism, and almost no serious Fascist political parties exist today. It is interesting to ponder what about Fascism united capitalists and Communists, democrats and socialists, the United States and the Soviet Union.

---

14 Gentile, p. 178.

· 17 ·

MIHAILO MARKOVIC

Neo-Marxism

Mihailo Markovic (b. 1923) is a leading representative of the Praxis school of Marxism. Markovic fought with the anti-Nazi resistance in Yugoslavia during World War II and subsequently taught philosophy at the University of Belgrade. His Praxis school draws upon Marx's "humanist" writings and it critical of both Western Capitalism and Soviet Communism. Yugoslavia's mixture of a planned socialist economy and decentralized worker-controlled business operating within a market is reflected in Markovic's ideals of democratic socialism. The Praxis school of Marxism has enjoyed much greater acceptance by Western leftists than Soviet Orthodoxy. Markovic has been a visiting Professor at the University of Michigan.

Markovic defines Praxis as the dialectially-related opposites of thought and action or the *critical activity* that appraises and transforms an incomplete or alienating reality from the perspective of an ideal. To do this one must recognize the interconnectedness of the seeming opposites of thought and action, real and ideal.

From this praxis perspective, Markovic attacks both unthinking activity and philosophy detached from reality and social action. Praxis seeks to synthesize the opposites of consciousness and action, real and ideal in one "total theoretico-practical being."[1]

> The awareness of an ideal is in the same time awareness of the limitation of the present mode of existence. Man cannot indefinitely bear the relative limitation and narrowness of any given mode of his being. This is why he rebels against compulsion, against alien institutions, and even his own patterns of behavior in the past. This is also the reason why he tends to change and to improve his social and natural surroundings, and his own style of life, in order to overcome those features of his life condition which he evaluates as limited and negative. However, man cannot evaluate anything as a limitation, or distinguish consistently between good and evil, between positive and negative, if he does not have any ideal, any consciousness of what ought to be in the future. In fact, a developed consciousness about the future directs man in his critique of the present. In this sense philosophy is always a *critical consciousness* with respect to any existing human situation.[2]

Human Nature

The primary ideal that Markovic believes man should strive for in changing the world is the ideal vision of human nature found in Marx's *Early Writings*. That nature is creative transformation of the world, through which man knows himself. Since such creativity is conditioned by different historical, social and economic conditions, man's nature is not fixed or constant.

> All possibilities are open in logic, but not in history. Human nature is not an abstract, fixed, transcendental entity. But neither is it something which can be created by any arbitrary decision of a free individual. In each historical epoch there is a general structure of human being, as a crystallization of the whole past history of human praxis. This structure is a concrete dynamic totality which underlies all of the more specific determinants, those of class, race, nation, religion, profession, and individual character. It is constituted by conflicting general features and tendencies of human behavior and thus it is dynamic and open for further change.[3]

Our contemporary habits, needs, potential powers, and aspirations are historical products. Human nature is not an abstract fixed, transcendental entity, nor is it something which can be created *anew* by an arbitrary decision of a free individual.

---

1   Mihailo Markovic, *From Affluence to Praxis: Philosophy and Social Criticism* (Ann Arbor, University of Michigan Press, 1974), p. 6.
2   Markovic, pp. 4–5.
3   Markovic, p. 209.

In each historical epoch there is a general structure which is a crystallization of the whole past history of human praxis. This structure is a concrete dynamic totality which underlies all more specific determinants—those of class, race, nation, religion, profession, and individual character. It is constituted by the opposite general features and tendencies of human behavior and therefore is dynamic and open for further change. We have to move within these natural, social and cultural limits. But within these limits a process of *self-determination* takes place. We choose among possibilities, we create new possibilities.[4]

For example, man appears to be acquisitive, possessive, greedy, egotistic, power-hungry under certain historical conditions characterized by private ownership of the means of production, commodity production, market competition and professional politics. For an uncritical, positivist, social philosophy this historically conditional picture of human actuality is the picture of human nature itself.[5]

So, Markovic's view of human nature is fluid: man is essentially creative, but is capable of many different, even contradictory behaviors, according to the social structure in which he lives.

...there are in man internal contradictions between positive and negative, good and evil, rational and irrational, desire for freedom and reluctance to assume responsibility, creative and destructive, social and egoistic, peaceful and aggressive. Both are human, and it is possible for these conflicting features to survive indefinitely. But it is also possible that man will act during a prolonged period of time in such a way that one would prevail over the other.[6]

Given the right social conditions, man's higher, nobler qualities will prevail.

Taking into account the great humanist tradition during the last twenty-five centuries as well as actual contemporary preferences which underlie all moral judgment, there can be little doubt that, *other conditions being equal*, and with all necessary qualifications and exceptions, there is a strong tendency to prefer freedom to slavery, creative action to destruction and passivity, consideration for general social needs to egoism, rationality to any behavior governed by blind emotional forces, and peacefulness to belligerency. It would be wrong and dogmatic to say that it is only these preferable qualities that constitute human *nature* or human *essence* or human *being*, as against another ontological level of human *appearance* to which all evil in man would be relegated. In order to establish a sense of direction and a

---

4 Markovic, p. 35.
5 Markovic, p. 12.
6 Markovic, p. 223.

general criterion of evaluation in a humanist philosophy and practice it is sufficient to claim that these qualities constitute what is most valuable in man and what can be considered the *optimal real potentiality* of human being. To fulfill these optimal potentialities is to live a "true," "genuine," "authentic," "humane" life. Failure to fulfill them is what is often called *alienation*.[7]

The task for Praxis school Marxists, therefore, is to create a society in which the best qualities of man are nurtured and allowed to develop. Such a society would liberate man's true nature or the "fundamental human capacities" of (1) unlimited sensory enjoyment; (2) reason; (3) imagination; (4) creativity; (5) communication; (6) social harmony and (7) true choice. Some examples of what Markovic means by these are:

> *Unlimited Development of the Senses.* Man can have an increasingly rich and manifold experience of the world. Our sensory powers may be magnified by the creation of suitable instruments. On the other hand, they can be refined by progressive cultivation and they can be liberated to the extent to which our surroundings become dereified. There is hardly any limit to the increase of our ability to see, to select, to interpret, to concentrate on one interesting dimension of our perceptive field, and to associate what we immediately perceive with a whole world....
>
> *The Ability to Harmonize Interests, Drives, and Aspirations* with those of other individuals. Without it men would not be able to live in a social community. Nevertheless, this faculty is very much blocked in social conditions favoring competition and struggle and the survival of the fittest.
>
> *Discrimination, Assessment, and Choice among Alternative Possibilities.* This faculty is the ground of human freedom. It can be actualized in a distorted way if an external authority (church, state, party) succeeds in imposing upon human individuals its own criteria of evaluation, its own conception of who they are and what they can be. That is why genuine human freedom coincides with the actualization of the capacity of *Self-Identification* and *Self-Consciousness*.
>
> A *Capacity for Communication*, not only in the sense of learning a language, but also in the sense of an increasing ability to understand the thoughts, feelings, desires, and motives of other persons who belong to other nations, classes, races, and cultures.[8]

---

7   Markovic, p. 7.
8   Markovic, pp. 13-14.

Thus, Markovic and the Praxis school of Marxism is very optimistic about the development of human capacities and social relations, given the correct social conditions.

Political Society

The goal of the Praxis school of Marxism is to criticize, in theory and practice, all existing social conditions that prevent the full realization of all human capacities, and to thereby create a new society that fulfills man's true nature. Praxis Marxism does not tolerate the existence of any situation that in any way alienates the individual; it is ceaseless in its criticism of all incomplete, imperfect social conditions and relations. It does not rest in its condemnation of any institution or relationship that inhibits man's freedom and happiness. This constantly critical stance, for Markovic, is itself pleasurable.

> In *praxis* self-realization is one of the essential moments: It IS the activity in which one actualizes the full wealth of his best potential capacities, an activity profoundly pleasurable for its own sake, no matter how much effort and energy it might require, no matter how pleasant its secondary effects such as success or prestige might be. Another essential characteristic of *praxis* is that, while involving self-affirmation, it also satisfies a need of other human beings. In the process of praxis man is immediately aware that, through his activity and/or its product he enriches the lives of others and indirectly becomes part of them. In labor and work this direct concern for another person's needs might be completely absent. The worker can be either completely self-oriented or concerned only about wages and success. Praxis involves a basic intuitive distinction between genuine and false needs. It also involves creativity, but in the broadest possible sense, which might include not only writing poetry, painting, dancing, projecting new architectural designs, composing music, or scientific research, but also teaching, playing, cooking, designing clothes, entertaining people, loving, raising children, and so forth.
>
> *Praxis* establishes valuable and warm links with other human beings: in such a way man becomes a *species being*, an individual who is in the same time a social being.
>
> *Praxis* is *universal* in the sense that man is able to incorporate in his activity the whole of nature and to reproduce the modes of action and production of all other living beings: man has learned from the bird how to fly and from the fish how to swim and dive; a man who belongs to a particular nation, class, race, region,

civilization is able to learn and assimilate in his activity the elements of activity of all other human beings....⁹

For Markovic, all humans are equally capable of such complete development-not just Plato's Philosopher-Kings or Aristotle's excellent men. Today, a worker-managed society like Yugoslavia's will realize that total human potential. Politics under such a system will be "deprofessionalized," as citizens of all kinds participate in self-government, taking turns holding authority.

> The existence of a moral and intellectual elite is *conditio sine qua non* of a really progressive and humanist social process. But it must not lead to the creation of a closed social group with special rights. There is a vast difference between a ruler who considers himself indispensable and uses force in order to make his subjects happier against their own will, and an ordinary competent man who, having temporarily left his profession to perform certain political functions, considers his office nothing more than an honor and uses force only against those who break democratically established norms of social behavior. Likewise there is a fundamental distinction between the *state* which has always been the coercive instrument of a particular social group whose interests it protected and promoted by force, and a truly democratic, social organization which needs force only to secure the general interests of the community against antisocial behavior of sick individuals. This type of truly democratic social organization is called *selfmanagement*....
>
> It would not be difficult to elect excellent deputies to hold office for a limited period of time from a larger number of gifted people in various professions who have acquired a certain political experience and skill. Strict responsibility to their voters, observance of democratic procedures in all decision-making, obligatory rotation of duties, lack of any material privileges (salaries for political functions should not exceed the pay scale for any other creative work), and various other measures should discourage any excessive political ambitions and effectively prevent their realization.¹⁰

As with Marx, Markovic sees the advancement of technology and the concomitant reduction of work as allowing everyone to participate in social self-governance.

> The decisive new historical fact relevant to these questions is that the considerable reduction of compulsory work and production, which will take place on a mass scale in an advanced future society, will liberate enormous human energies

---

9 Markovic, pp. 65-66.
10 Markovic, pp. 86-87.

and talents for political life. The general education and culture, including political knowledge of these potential political "amateurs," need not be inferior to that of "professionals." By participating in local communal life and in various voluntary organizations, many of them have acquired a satisfactory experience in public relations and the art of management.[11]

Both involve concentrations of wealth and power and must be overthrown if human potential is to be realized.

Social Ethics

In Praxis Marxism, the source of human evil is not the individual, but social conditions. If social conditions are humanized, people will be good. If the social system becomes perfect, human beings will become perfect.

> Marx's early anthropological writings lead to the conclusion that evil is excluded from his concepts of *human essence* and *human nature* and referred to a historically transient phase of alienation. As long as private property and exploitation still exist, and relations among men are still dominated by selfishness, greed, envy, and aggressiveness, man is alienated from his essence. These negative features of empirical man—such as they have existed so far in history—are not part of human nature; as long as they characterize human relations man is not yet truly human. However, "communism is the positive abolition of *private property*, of *human self-alienation*, and this is the *real appropriation of human* nature through and for man. It is, therefore, the return of man himself as a *social*, i.e., really *human* being, a complete and conscious return which assimilates all the wealth of previous development."[12]

The evil that we see in people today can be attributed to the oppressive social system in which they live, the removal of which will liberate people's kinder attributes.

> In general, the scarcity, weakness, lack of freedom, social and national insecurity, a feeling of inferiority, emptiness, and poverty to which the vast majority of people are condemned, give rise to such mechanisms of defense and compensation as national and class hatred, egoism, escape from responsibility, and aggressive and destructive behavior. Many present-day forms of evil really could be overcome in a society which would provide to each individual satisfaction of his basic vital needs, liberation from compulsory routine work, immediate participation in

---

11 Markovic, p. 231.
12 Markovic, pp. 218-219.

decision-making, a relatively free access to the sources of information, prolonged education, a possibility of appropriating genuine cultural values, and the protection of fundamental human rights.[13]

The real source of contemporary social problems is the concentration of economic and political power in the hands of a few and the corollary lack of participation in economic and political decision-making by the many.

> Almost all contemporary forms of alienation are rooted in the existence of social groups which have a monopoly on economic and political power. This monopoly itself is based either on the private ownership of the means of production (in the case of the capitalist class) or on the privileged position in the political organization of the society (in the case of bureaucracy), or both. To be sure, monopoly implies various kinds of usurpation. The usurpation of the unpaid work of other people is usually called *exploitation*. The usurpation of other people's rights in the social decision-making is *political hegemony*.[14]

Therefore, the only ethical thing to do is to overthrow those social systems which concentrate power in the hands of the few and exclude the many. The good per son, according to Markovic, critically assesses all social organizations and relations that prevent the realization of full human capacities and leads revolutionary movements that smash those oppressive institutions, establishing just, participatory, humanized societies in which all will be in control of their lives, fulfilled and happy.

> Therefore, to *humanize radically* the contemporary world means to create conditions in which each individual can participate in the control of the enormous social and technical forces which man has at his disposal. An essential condition of such fundamental human liberation is the *abolition of any concentration of political and economic power in the hands of any particular social group*.

> The abolition (*Aufhebung*) of private ownership the means of production and the abolition of capitalists as a class is the first decisive step in this direction. The abolition of politics as a profession which enables a social group permanently to control social operations, and the abolition of bureaucracy as a privileged elite is the second decisive step. Each is *a necessary condition* of a radical humanization, but only both taken together constitute its sufficient condition.[15]

---

13 Markovic, p. 225.
14 Markovic, p. 79.
15 Markovic, p. 81.

Despite the waning of interest in Marxism in the 1980's, Markovic's Praxis theory is important for the themes it raises. The Rousseauist identification of human evil and unhappiness with "society" has had a powerful impact on contemporary Western society. A criminal's destructive conduct and an artist's beautiful creation are not their own responsibility, but are the result of social structures and relations. A conservative shift in the West recently has tempered this view and placed greater responsibility on the individual for his actions, but this blaming "society" for individual conduct remains a strong tendency in America. Also, Markovic's emphasis on "participation" in social decision-making by the masses of people has been taken over by many non-communist thinkers. Whether it be the General Motors management that encourages auto workers to participate in the design and marketing of cars or the U. S. Catholic Bishops urging popular participation in political and ecclesiastical institutions, participation has become a key concept in contemporary life. Benjamin Barber constructs an entire political theory on political participation, drawing on Aristotle, Rousseau and Jefferson.

Both the tendency to identify individual evil and unhappiness with social conditions and the trend of participation in social management, raise important questions for the immediate future of political theory. For example, is the human individual in any way distinct regardless of social circumstances? Is there, as in St. Augustine's conceptions of sin and redemption, any constant in human nature? Or, do the transcendent ethics of Christianity's City of God provide an independent standard of reference for man, regardless of social circumstances? Can society fully liberate man from all evil and pain? And, can all people participate in all social decisions that affect their lives? If not, how do we decide to divide up the responsibilities? Should everyone participate in everything or merely have the option to do so, and how can either choice be made available? Could either be oppressive? Finally, if capitalist society (or a mixed economy in the case of most Western regimes) causes all the alienation that people suffer from, will its replacement by socialism eliminate all alienation? Markovic seems to think so. Why didn't it work out that way in the Soviet Union? And, can any of those essential human capacities (free creativity, full sensory enjoyment, positive social relations) be realized in a capitalist, market society? If so, why? I do not know the answers to these questions, but I suspect political theory will be preoccupied with them for the next fifty years.

· 18 ·

HANNAH ARENDT

The Human Condition

Hannah Arendt (1906-1975) was a German philosopher who fled Germany in the 1930's during the Nazi persecution of Jews. She settled in America and joined the Faculty, with other German intellectuals, of "The University in Exile" in New York City (later The Graduate Faculty of The New School for Social Research). She lectured on political philosophy at Princeton and the University of Chicago. Arendt's The Human Condition is the clearest expression of her own political theory, though she wrote extensively on politics, especially the rise of Totalitarianism in the twentieth century.

Hannah Arendt's political theory is distinctive for criticizing both dominant schools of twentieth century thought: Communism and liberalism. She critiques both Western democracies and Communist societies from the perspective of the Greek Classics, especially Aristotle.

Human Nature

Arendt describes human nature in terms of the *vita activa*, or "life activity" distinctive to mankind. She divides human activities into three categories: (1) Labor; (2) Work; and (3) Action.

Labor is the activity that humans engage in to satisfy their physical needs, to earn the material necessities of life. Our "job" is our labor. It is the "sweat of our brow" that is expended to secure the things we need to stay alive.

Work, by contrast, is interacting with the material world not for mere survival, but to create something permanent in the world as an expression of one's identity. Architecture, music, scientific discovery, art, literature, film all express the unique personality of their creator, and so, the creator and others know him through that creation in work. Arendt thus makes a distinction ignored by Marx between Labor, carried on for necessity, and Work, carried on by choice; Labor that is simply a means to another end (survival) and Work that is an end in itself.

Action, by contrast with both Labor and Work involves human interaction with other humans. Action, for Arendt, is relations between individuals in ways unrelated to economics. The sources of human Action are the faculties of reasoned speech and moral choice-those human abilities that Aristotle identified with politics.

> All three activities and their corresponding conditions are intimately connected with the most general condition of human existence: birth and death, natality and mortality. Labor assures not only individual survival, but the life of the species. Work and its product, the human artifact, bestow a measure of permanence and durability upon the futility of mortal life and the fleeting character of human time. Action, in so far as it engaged in founding and preserving political bodies, creates the condition for remembrance, that is, for history.[1]

For Arendt, these three human activities form a natural hierarchy with the faculties of reasoned speech and moral choice superior to the economic activities of labor and work. This hierarchy corresponds to Aristotle's hierarchy of "public" and "private," the former being the realm of freedom and the latter the realm of necessity.

The exercise of man's unique faculties in reasoned speech and moral choice in the small deliberative communities of the Greek polis, for Arendt, is the highest human activity. The life of economics, by contrast, is tied to our lower natures, our private senses and the physical needs we share with the beasts. Although Labor and Work are necessary aspects of human life, they are not the noblest, most human aspects and therefore, someone solely concerned with

---

1 Hannah Arendt, *The Human Condition* (Chicago, University of Chicago Press, 1958), pp. 8-9.

economics is *enslaved* to their lower natures. A life devoted to making money and consuming is a kind of slavery.

> Aristotle distinguished three ways of life (*bioi*) which men might choose in freedom, that is, in full independence of the necessities of life and the relationships they originated. This prerequisite of freedom ruled out all ways of life chiefly devoted to keeping one's self alive—not only labor, which was the way of life of the slave, who was coerced by the necessity to stay alive and by the rule of his master, but also the working life of the free craftsman and the acquisitive life of the merchant. In short, it excluded everybody who involuntarily or voluntarily, for his whole life or temporarily, had lost the free disposition of his movements and activities. The remaining three ways of life have in common that they were concerned with the "beautiful," that is, with things neither necessary nor merely useful: the life of enjoying bodily pleasures in which the beautiful, as it is given, is consumed; the life devoted to the matters of the *polis*, in which excellence produces beautiful deeds; and the life of the philosopher devoted to inquiry into, and contemplation of, things eternal, whose ever-lasting beauty can neither be brought about through the producing interference of man nor be changed through his consumption of them.[2]

The problem with our twentieth-century world, for Arendt, is that all nations, capitalist and Communist, are "slaves" in this sense: they are obsessed with economic progress to the exclusion of man's higher activities. The value of all activities is measured in terms of "productivity"; any human quality (such as contemplation or deliberation) that impairs the profitability of the corporation or efficiency of the economy are denounced and discarded by modern society. All activities are judged according to their market value. This sounds like Marx's critique of capitalism, but Arendt aims it at both capitalist and Communist societies.

Political Society

The public realm, for Arendt, properly serves and enhances man's unique faculties of reasoned speech and moral choice in the public deliberation of the community. The private realm of economics is relegated to the Household, which properly takes care of man's physical needs (including emotional comfort and intimacy).

The problem with twentieth-century "Society" is that it takes the private (economic) and projects it onto the public realm, effectively destroying both.

---

2   Arendt, pp. 12-13.

The "socialization" of private economic life-from mass production to mass consumption, ruins both the public and the private realms, distorting man's higher and lower natures. Taking man's private needs and desires (from eating breakfast to making love) and projecting them onto the "Society," while reducing the public realm of politics to private interest and personal greed turns the natural hierarchy of human activity upside down. True politics requires the public deliberation of reasonable minds rising above the private concerns of property and wealth; true economics require the comfort and security of the household. Modern society, for Arendt, provides neither. Increasingly, our most private needs are satisfied by the market and our most cherished public institutions are debased by private interest and greed.

> In the modern world, the social and the political realms are much less distinct. That politics is nothing but a function of society, that action, speech, and thought are primarily superstructures upon social interest, is not a discovery of Karl Marx but on the contrary is among the axiomatic assumptions Marx accepted uncritically from the political economists of the modern age. This functionalization makes it impossible to perceive any serious gulf between the two realms; and this is not a matter of a theory or an ideology, since with the rise of society, that is, the rise of the "household" (*oikia*) or of economic activities to the public realm, housekeeping and all matters pertaining formerly to the private sphere of the family have become a "collective" concern.[3]

Social Ethics

For Arendt, the good society would develop man's highest ethical and rational qualities and satisfy his economic needs properly. Good social relations involve respecting those distinctive needs and abilities and not convoluting them, as is done in Modern Society.

The public deliberation that exercises man's reasoned speech and moral choice is important because the individual reveals his unique personality in such activity and is affirmed in that identity by others.

> In acting and speaking, men show who they are, reveal actively their unique personal identities and thus make their appearance in the human world, while their physical identities appear without any activity of their own in the unique shape of the body and sound of the voice. This disclosure of "who" in contradistinction to "what" somebody is—his qualities, gifts, talents, and short-comings, which he may

---

3   Arendt, p. 133.

display or hide—is implicit in everything somebody says and does. It can be hidden only in complete silence and perfect passivity, but its disclosure can almost never be achieved as a willful purpose, as though one possessed and could dispose of this "who" in the same manner he has and can dispose of his qualities. On the contrary, it is more than likely that the "who," which appears so clearly and unmistakably to others, remains hidden from the person himself, like the *daimon* in Greek religion which accompanies each man throughout his life, always looking over his shoulder from behind and thus visible only to those he encounters.

This revelatory quality of speech and action comes to the fore where people are *with* others and neither for nor against them—that is, in sheer human togetherness. Although nobody knows whom he reveals when he disclosed himself in deed or word, he must be willing to risk the disclosure, and this neither the doer of good works, who must be without self and preserve complete anonymity, nor the criminal, who must hide himself from others, can take upon themselves.[4]

The *polis* was supposed to multiply the occasions to win "immortal fame," that is, to multiply the chances for everybody to distinguish himself, to show in deed and word who he was in his unique distinctness. One, if not the chief, reason for the incredible development of gift and genius in Athens, as well as for the hardly less surprising swift decline of the city-state, was precisely that from the beginning to end its foremost aim was to make the extraordinary an ordinary occurrence of everyday life.[5]

Modern, mass society destroys man's ability to reveal his unique identity by replacing small communities with mass culture and by elevating economics to the premier public concern. Modern capitalist and communist society tells people that they will know themselves through production and consumption of material goods. But such lower activity, charged Arendt, does not have the ability to reveal or affirm the individual's unique identity as does the small deliberative community. This explains, for her, the alienation and despair of Modern life, despite tremendous material abundance. And, such a deprived existence leads to masses of people following charismatic political leaders (such as Hitler and Stalin) that establish totalitarian regimes. More recently, the rise of religious cults, drug use and suicide, Arendt would attribute to the alienation spawned by a lack of affirmed identity in rational communities.

---

4   Arendt, pp. 179-180.
5   Arendt, p. 197.

> We saw before that in the rise of society it was ultimately the life of the species which asserted itself. Theoretically, the turning point from the earlier modern age's insistence on the "egoistic" life of the individual to its later emphasis on "social" life an "socialized man" (Marx) came when Marx transformed the cruder notion of classical economy—that all men, in so far as they act at all, act for reasons of self-interest—into forces of interest which inform, move, and direct the classes of society, and through their conflicts direct society as a whole. Socialized mankind is that state of society where only one interest rules, and the subject of this interest is either classes or mankind, but neither man or men. The point is that now even the last trace of action in what men were doing, the motive implied in self-interest, disappeared. What was left was a "natural force," the force of the life process itself, to which all men and all human activities were equally submitted ("the thought process itself is a natural process") and whose only aim, if it had an aim at all, was survival of the animal species man. None of the higher capacities of man was any longer necessary to connect individual life with the life of the species; individual life became part of the life process, and to labor, to assure the continuity of one's own life and the life of his family, was all that was needed. What was not needed, not necessitated by life's metabolism with nature, was either superfluous or could be justified only in terms of a peculiarity of human as distinguished from other animal life—so that Milton was considered to have written his *Paradise Lost* for the same reasons and out of similar urges that compel the silkwork to produce silk.[6]

Despite Modern World Alienation, which technology will soon liberate into "a society of laborers,"[7] Arendt remains optimistic about the possibilities in human life. People will always retain the ability to act humanly, to develop reason, speech and ethics affirmed by others. Even in a mass society that throws individuals into large organizations and a mass economy that trivializes and debases their needs, people are capable of forming affirming communities.

> The *polis*, properly speaking, is not the city-state in its physical location; it is the organization of the people as it arises out of acting and speaking together, and its true space lies between people living together for this purpose, no matter where they happen to be. "Wherever you go, you will be a *polis*": these famous words became not merely the watchword of Greek colonization, they expressed the conviction that action and speech create a space between the participants which can find its proper location almost any time and anywhere.[8]

---

6 Arendt, p. 321.
7 Arendt, p. 5.
8 Arendt, p. 198.

It may occur in a small town or on one floor of a large apartment building; it may emerge unpredictably in a small college or a small group of students in a large university. Possibly a church or a corporation or a government office will spawn such an affirming community, where the individuals will reveal their distinctive personalities to others and to themselves. The human faculty of Action is always possible, despite the Modern world's attempt to destroy it. Hannah Arendt took hope from the emergence of new communities in society, especially in America.

· 19 ·

ROBERT NOZICK

Libertarian

Robert Nozick (b. 1938) is a professor of Philosophy at Harvard University and a leading representative of "libertarian" political thought. His principal work, *Anarchy, State and Utopia*, claims to provide a philosophical argument for contemporary conservative ideology, with its emphasis on individual liberty, strictly limited government, reduced taxes, deregulation of business, etc. Written in 1974, this book seems prophetic of the rise of conservative government in both the United States and Britain.

Human Nature

Nozick accepts John Locke's conception of man as a naturally "free, equal and independent" individual possessing Natural Rights to "Life, Liberty and Property."[1] As he writes in the first sentences of *Anarchy, State and Utopia*:

---

1   Robert Nozick, *Anarchy, State and Utopia* (New York, Basic Books, 1974), p. 10.

> Individuals have rights, and there are things no person or group may do to them (without violating their rights). So strong and far-reaching are these rights that they raise the question of what, if anything, the state and its officials may do.[2]

Part of the popular appeal of Nozick's ideas is that he does not go into great depth in his exposition, and this is certainly the case with his conception of Human Nature. Nozick simply repeats Locke's assertion, without elaborating the materialist underpinnings or philosophical implications of Locke's conception of man's nature. Nozick's analysis also reveals an unawareness of the several critiques of this view of Human Nature, from St. Thomas Aquinas to Karl Marx.

As such, Nozick's theory is popular with the non-intellectual sectors of society, particularly the political Right. But, as we shall see, his philosophy is particularly useful to contemporary conservatism.

Political Society

Again repeating Lockean liberalism, Nozick proposes a state limited to protecting individual rights to Life, Liberty and Property. This Nozick calls the "minimalist state" because it performs the bare minimum of duties. Nozick is especially careful to assert what the state should *not* do:

> Our main conclusions about the state are that a minimal state, limited to the narrow functions of protection against force, theft, fraud, enforcement of contracts, and so on, is justified; that any more extensive state will violate persons' rights not to be forced to do certain things, and is unjustified; and that the minimal state is inspiring as well as right. Two noteworthy implications are that the state may not use its coercive apparatus for the purpose of getting some citizens to aid others, or in order to prohibit activities to people for their *own* good or protection.[3]

This formulation of the best state established Nozick as a leader of Libertarian thought and forms his critique of the American Welfare State. Its two basic tenets are that the government should not tax some (wealthy) people to aid other (poor) people, and that the state should not prohibit activities and substances (e.g., prostitution and drugs) to protect people from themselves (so-called "victimless" crimes). The underlying assumption is that individuals

---

2   Nozick, p. ix.
3   Nozick, p. ix.

are essentially free and independent of others and society, and therefore should not be held responsible for others or have others responsible for them. So long as one does not violate the rights of others, he does not have to have anything to do with them, unless he freely contracts to do so. Man is not naturally social, but naturally solitary, free and independent.

Nozick's argument against taxing some citizens to support others is, again, derived from Locke's theory of private property (see Chapter 9). In it, legitimate title to property comes from the mixing of one's labor with nature (the "labor theory of value"). The property gotten from this effort becomes one's right, and the State is established to protect rights. The government may legitimately tax citizens' property to cover the costs of protecting their rights, but not to transfer their money to other citizens. Nozick argues that the American Welfare State violates this proper role of government through an "Entitlement Theory" that every citizen is entitled to an income, whether they earn it or not.

> The minimal state is the most extensive state that can be justified. Any state more extensive violates people's rights. Yet many persons have put forth reasons purporting to justify a more extensive state.[4]

> The legitimacy of altering social institutions to achieve greater equality of material condition is, though often assumed, rarely *argued* for. Writers note that in a given country the wealthiest n percent of the population holds more than that percentage of the wealth, and the poorest n percent holds less; that to get to the wealth of the top n percent from the poorest, one must look at the bottom p percent (where p is vastly greater than n), and so forth. They then proceed immediately to discuss how this might be altered. On the entitlement conception of justice in holdings, one *cannot* decide whether the state must do something to alter the situation merely by looking at a distributional profile or at facts such as these. It depends upon how the distribution came about. Some processes yielding these results would be legitimate, and the various parties would be entitled to their respective holdings. If these distributional facts *did* arise by a legitimate process, then they themselves are legitimate. This is, of course, *not* to say that they may not be changed, provided this can be done without violating people's entitlements.[5]

An obvious example of this is the frequent description of wealth distribution in poor, Third World countries, where we hear that 90% of the wealth is owned by 5% of the population (and immediately try to devise ways to distribute wealth more evenly). Nozick argues that it is not the distribution of wealth that is

---

4   Nozick, p. 149.
5   Nozick, p. 232.

important, but how that distribution took place. If the wealthy 5% earned that wealth through labor or free contract it is perfectly legitimate, as he shows in his famous "Wilt Chamberlain" example.

> Now suppose that Wilt Chamberlain is greatly in demand by basketball teams, being a great gate attraction. (Also suppose contracts run only for a year, with players being free agents.) He signs the following sort of contract with a team: In each home game, twenty-five cents from the price of each ticket of admission goes to him. (We ignore the question of whether he is "gouging" the owners, letting them look out for themselves.) The season starts, and people cheerfully attend his team's games; they buy their tickets, each time dropping a separate twenty-five cents of their admission price into a special box with Chamberlain's name on it. They are excited about seeing him play; it is worth the total admission price to them. Let us suppose that in one season one million persons attend his home games, and Wilt Chamberlain winds up with $250,000, a much larger sum than the average income and larger even than anyone else has. Is he entitled to this income? Is this new distribution D_2 unjust? If so, why? There is no question about whether each of the people was entitled to the control over the resources they held in D_1; because that was the distribution (your favorite) that (for the purposes of argument) we assumed was acceptable. Each of these persons chose to give twenty-five cents of their money to Chamberlain. They could have spent it on going to the movies, or on candy bars, or on copies of *Dissent* magazine, or of *Monthly Review*. But they all, at least one million of them, converged on giving it to Wilt Chamberlain in exchange for watching him play basketball.[6]

For Nozick, everyone is like Wilt Chamberlain, in having a talent that can be sold on the market. In the best society, they will be left free to sell themselves and fully enjoy the profits. The hardworking, talented people will become wealthy and not have to worry about the state taxing all their income and giving it to the poor. The poor, for Nozick, are not "victims" of "exploitation," but either lazy or untalented, or both. It is unjust to punish the good (hardworking, talented, rich) people by taxing much of their income and giving it to the poor (lazy, untalented) people. The source of current unjust, Welfare State and socialist redistribution of wealth is the envy of the poor, disguised as the ideal of equality.

> It is plausible to connect equality with self-esteem. The envious person, if he cannot (also) possess a thing (talent, and so on) that someone else has, prefers that the

---

6   Nozick, p. 101.

other person not have it either. The envious man prefers neither one having it, to the other's having it and his not having it.[7]

Here I prefer to focus on the *strangeness* of the emotion of envy. Why do some people *prefer* that others not have their better score on some dimension, rather than being pleased at another's being well-off or having good fortune; why don't They at least just shrug it off?

....How can another's activities, or characteristics, affect one's own self-esteem? Shouldn't my self-esteem, feeling of worth, and so forth, depend only upon facts about me? If it is me that I'm evaluating in some way, how *can* facts about other persons play a role? The answer, of course, is that we evaluate how *well* we do something by comparing our performance to others, to what others can do.[8]

Also, Nozick does not subscribe to the Marxist view (see Chapter 13) that the poverty of the lower classes is due to their exploitation by the rich.

This question is of importance for what remains of Marxist economic theory. With the crumbling of the labor theory of value, the underpinning of its particular theory of exploitation dissolves. And the charm and simplicity of this theory's *definition* of exploitation is lost when it is realized that according to the definition there will be exploitation in *any* society in which investment takes place for a greater future product (perhaps because of population growth); and in *any* society in which those unable to work, or to work productively, are *subsidized* by the labor of others.[9]

Nozick, rather, argues that the lower class people may not have the intelligence or abilities to improve their lot. And if the capitalist businesses were turned over to the workers, they would very soon require the same talents that the capitalists needed to get rich.

The workers may lack the entrepreneurial ability to identify promising opportunities for profitable activity, and to organize firms to respond to these opportunities. In this case, the workers can try to *hire* entrepreneurs and managers to start a firm for them and then turn the authority functions over to the workers (who are the owners) after one year. (Though, as Kirzner emphasizes, entrepreneurial alertness would also be needed in deciding whom to hire.) Different groups of workers would compete for entrepreneurial talent, bidding up the price of such services, while entrepreneurs with capital attempted to hire workers under traditional

---

7   Nozick, p. 239.
8   Nozick, p. 240.
9   Nozick, p. 253.

ownership arrangements. Let us ignore the question of what the equilibrium in this market would look like to ask why groups of workers aren't doing this now.

> It's *risky* starting a new firm. One can't identify easily new entrepreneurial talent, and much depends on estimates of future demand and of availability of resources, on unforeseen obstacles, on change, and so forth. Specialized investment institutions and sources of venture capital develop to run just these risks. Some persons don't want to run these risks of investing or backing new ventures, or starting ventures themselves. Capitalist society allows the separation of the bearing of these risks from other activities. The workers in the Edsel branch of the Ford Motor Company did not bear the risks of the venture, and when it lost money they did not pay back a portion of their salary.[10]

So, the best society is a laissez-faire free market capitalism with a government that protects the benefits of that system. Today, Nozick might explain the major Communist nations' (Soviet and Chinest) return to market principles, decentralized management and profit incentives as recognition of the truths of his theory.

Utopia

However, Nozick admits that his endorsement of old-fashioned laissez-faire American capitalism is not as inspiring as St. Augustine's City of God of perfect justice and peace or Marx's Communism of perfect freedom and equality. So, Nozick argues that in his perfect society, people inclined towards such utopian visions of man and society will be free to organize any kind of community they wish. If a group of people voluntarily wish to live as Communists, abolishing private property and sharing everything, they are free, in Nozick's society, to buy a farm in Vermont and set up a commune.

> In *our* actual world, what corresponds to the model of possible worlds is a wide and diverse range of communities which people can enter if they are admitted, leave if they wish to, shape according to their wishes; a society in which utopian experimentation can be tried, different styles of life can be lived, and alternative visions of the good can be individually or jointly pursued.[11]

---

10   Nozick, p. 255.
11   Nozick, p. 307.

Such freedom of association will spawn a wonderful variety of communities, satisfying many talents and interests of individuals.

> The first route begins with the fact that people are different. They differ in temperament, interests, intellectual ability, aspirations, natural bent, spiritual quests, and the kind of life they wish to lead. They diverge in the values they have and have different weightings for the values they share. (They wish to live in different climates—some in mountains, plains, deserts, seashores, cities, towns.) There is no reason to think that there is *one* community which will serve as ideal for all people and much reason to think that there is not.
>
> The conclusion to draw is that there will not be *one* kind of community existing and one kind of life led in utopia. Utopia will consist of utopias, of many different and divergent communities in which people lead different kinds of lives under different institutions. Some kinds of communities will be more attractive to most than others; communities will wax and wane. People will leave some for others or spend their whole lives in one. Utopia is a framework for utopias, a place where people are at liberty to join together voluntarily to pursue and attempt to realize their own vision of the good life in the ideal community but where no one can *impose* his own utopian vision upon others....Different communities, each with a slightly different mix, will provide a range from which each individual can choose that community which best approximates *his* balance among competing values. (Its opponents will call this the smorgasbord conception of utopia, preferring restaurants with only one dinner available, or, rather, preferring a one-restaurant town with one item on the menu.)[12]

Nozick's design for utopia is thus premised on the Lockean conception of man as a sensory being with different physical desires and definitions of good. Society should reflect this variety. There is no objective good, in God's Law or Aristotle's Golden Mean or Marx's "Species being."

Social Ethics

The one good, for Nozick, therefore, is the negative ethics of respecting others' individual rights and preferences, and otherwise leaving them alone. The only legitimate interference with the individual is when he violates another's rights, in which case the injured person is deserving of compensation. Determining

---

12 Nozick, pp. 309–310.

and awarding such compensation is the proper role of the State, through the Courts.

> A line (or hyper-plane) circumscribes an area in moral space around an individual. Locke holds that this line is determined by an individual's natural rights, which limit the action of others. Non-Lockeans view other considerations as setting the position and contour of the line. In any case the following question arises: *Are others forbidden to perform actions that transgress the boundary or encroach upon the circumscribed area, or are they permitted to perform such actions provided that they compensate the person whose boundary has been crossed?* Unravelling this question will occupy us for much of this chapter. Let us say that a system forbids an action to a person if it imposes (is geared to impose) some penalty upon him for doing the act, in addition to exacting compensation from him for the act's victims. Something fully compensates a person for a loss if and only if it makes him no worse off than he otherwise would have been; it compensates person X for person Y's action A if X is no worse off receiving it, Y having done A, than X would have been without receiving it if Y had not done A....A person may choose to do himself, I shall suppose, the things that would impinge across his boundaries when done without his consent by another. (Some of these things may be impossible for him to do to himself.) Also, he may give another permission to do these things to him (including things impossible for him to do to himself.) Voluntary consent opens the border for crossings. Locke, of course, would hold that there are things others may not do to you by your permission; namely, those things you have no right to do to yourself. Locke would hold that your giving your permission cannot make it morally permissible for another to kill you, because you have no right to commit suicide. My nonpaternalistic position holds that someone may choose (or permit another) to do so himself *anything*, unless he has acquired an obligation to some third party not to do or allow it.[13]

---

13 Nozick, pp. 57–58.

· 20 ·

JOHN RAWLS

American Liberalism

John Rawls (b. 1921) is a professor of Philosophy at Harvard University. Born in Baltimore, he was educated at Princeton. Rawls' *Theory of Justice* is perhaps the most significant book in American political theory in the past 25 years. Written in 1971, it has provoked literally dozens of articles in scholarly journals and several books.

Rawls' *Theory of Justice* has had a tremendous impact because it begins with traditional liberal Social Contract theory, but concludes that a just government is more intrusive than John Locke's state limited to protecting private rights. As Nozick has been seen as the philosopher of the Conservative Right, Rawls' theory has been perceived as providing a philosophical justification for Welfare State Liberalism.

Rawls' *Theory of Justice* answers the question: what kind of political society would a purely rational person choose? To create the conditions for such rational choice, Rawls places man in an "original position" (like Hobbes or Locke's "State of Nature") behind a "veil of ignorance" as to where in society one will eventually end up. Not knowing if one will be prominent or obscure, rich or poor, advantaged or disadvantaged, would cause one to choose a "maximin" strategy, or create a society in which the worst possible outcome is better than the worst possible outcome of any other society. Thus, the "Maximin" approach maximizes the minimum or serves the most disadvantaged better than any other social system. Such an arrangement, according to Rawls, would establish a system of "justice as fairness."

Rawls' conception of "justice as fairness" rests upon two principles:

(1) Society should allow the greatest individual liberty compatible with the same liberty for others. This is the classical British liberal statement (Locke's Law of Nature) that allows complete individual freedom so long as it does not violate the similar rights of others (to life, liberty and property).

(2) Any inequalities of wealth must work out to the benefit of the poorest (with the proviso that any elimination of inequality by the State would harm the interests of the poorest). This principle reflects the argument that some inequality can benefit all, including the poorest, as, for example, brilliant managers who can render all production more efficient commanding higher salaries.

The maximin strategy produced by the rational person in the original position behind the veil of ignorance would produce these two principles of justice: individual liberty compatible with that of others and inequality so long as it benefits the most disadvantaged.[1]

Human Nature

Rawls actually denies that he has or needs a theory of Human Nature for his Theory of Justice. In a recent article in *Philosophy and Public Affairs*, Rawls asserts that he wishes to avoid "claims to universal truth, or claims about the essential nature and identity of persons."[2] Yet there remains an implicit theory of Human Nature in the first principle of justice: perfect individual liberty constrained only by the rights of others assumes a Lockean, "free, equal and independent" man. Rawls' own description of man appears in his discussion of the "circumstances of justice." Man there is a self-interested individual who enters society for its material benefits the classic Lockean formulation (see Chapter 9).

> The circumstances of justice may be described as the normal conditions under which human cooperation is both possible and necessary. Thus, as I noted at the outset, although a society is a cooperative venture for mutual advantage, it is typically marked by a conflict as well as an identity of interests. There is an identity of interests since social cooperation makes possible a better life for all than any would

---

1   John Rawls, *A Theory of Justice* (Cambridge, Harvard University Press, 1971).
2   John Rawls, "Justice as Fairness: Political not Metaphysical," *Philosophy and Public Affairs*, Summer 1985, p. 223.

have if each were to try to live solely by his own efforts. There is a conflict of interests since men are not indifferent as to how the greater benefits produced by their collaborations are distributed, for in order to pursue their ends they each prefer a larger to a lesser share. Thus principles are needed for choosing among the various social arrangements which determine this division of advantages and for underwriting an agreement on the proper distributive shares. These requirements define the role of justice. The background conditions that give rise to these necessities are the circumstances of justice.

These conditions may be divided into two kinds. First, there are the objective circumstances which make human cooperation both possible and necessary. Thus, many individuals coexist together at the same time on a definite geographical territory. These individuals are roughly similar in physical and mental powers; or at any rate, their capacities are comparable in that no one among them can dominate the rest. They are vulnerable to attack, and all are subject to having their plans blocked by the united force of others. Finally, there is the condition of moderate scarcity understood to cover a wide range of situations. Natural and other resources are not so abundant that schemes of cooperation become superfluous, nor are conditions so harsh that fruitful ventures must inevitably break down. While mutually advantageous arrangements are feasible, the benefits they yield fall short of the demands men put forward.

The subjective circumstances are the relevant aspects of the subjects of cooperation, that is, of the persons working together. Thus while the parties have roughly similar needs and interests, or needs and interests in various ways complementary, so that mutually advantageous cooperation among them is possible, they nevertheless have their own plans of life. These plans, or conceptions of the good, lead them to have different ends and purposes, and to make conflicting claims on the natural and social resources available. Moreover, although the interests advanced by these plans are not assumed to be interests in the self, they are the interests of a self that regards its conception of the good as worthy of recognition and that advances claims in its behalf as deserving satisfaction. I shall emphasize this aspect of the circumstances of justice by assuming that the parties take no interest in one another's interests. I also suppose that men suffer from various shortcomings of knowledge, thought, and judgment. Their knowledge is necessarily incomplete, their powers of reasoning, memory, and attention are always limited, and their judgment is likely to be distorted by anxiety, bias, and a preoccupation with their own affairs. Some of these defects spring from moral faults, from selfishness and negligence; but to a large degree, they are simply part of men's natural situation. As a consequence individuals not only have different plans of life but there exists a diversity of philosophical and religious belief, and of political and social doctrines.

> Now this constellation of conditions I shall refer to as the circumstances of justice.[3]

And, Rawls' "rational" man in the original position is rational in the British liberal sense of calculating material self-interest.

> As I have said, moral personality is characterized by two capacities: one for a conception of the good, the other for a sense of justice. When realized, the first is expressed by a rational plan of life, the second by a regulative desire to act upon certain principles of right. Thus a moral person is a subject with ends he has chosen, and his fundamental preference is for conditions that enable him to frame a mode of life that expresses his nature as a free and equal rational being as fully as circumstances permit. Now the unity of the person is manifest in the coherence of his plan, this unity being founded on the higherorder desire to follow, in ways consistent with his sense of right and justice, the principles of rational choice.[4]

Political Society

The political society resulting from Rawls' principles of justice bears a striking resemblance to the American Welfare State. It is premised on a Constitutional democracy which guarantees individual liberty (especially of speech, press and political participation); it has a capitalist market economy, but regulates social opportunities—especially through taxation and education.

> The liberal interpretation of the two principles seeks, then, to mitigate the influence of social contingencies and natural for tune on distributive shares. To accomplish this end it is necessary to impose further basic structural conditions on the social system. Free market arrangements must be set within a framework of political and legal institutions which regulates the overall trends of economic events and preserves the social conditions necessary for fair equality of opportunity. The elements of this framework are familiar enough, though it may be worthwhile to recall the importance of preventing excessive accumulations of property and wealth and of maintaining equal opportunities of education for all. Chances to acquire cultural knowledge and skills should not depend upon one's class position, and so the school system, whether public or private, should be designed to even out class barriers.[5]

---

3 Rawls, *A Theory of Justice*, pp. 126-127.
4 Rawls, *A Theory of Justice*, p. 561.
5 Rawls, *A Theory of Justice*, p. 73.

Rawlsian justice, then, differs from Nozick's Libertarianism in acknowledging the effects of social circumstances on individuals and requiring the state to compensate for differences in economic opportunities.

> Perhaps some will think that the person with greater natural endowments deserves those assets and the superior character that made their development possible. Because he is more worthy in this sense, he deserves the greater advantages that he could achieve with them. This view, however, is surely incorrect. It seems to be one of the fixed points of our considered judgments that no one deserves his place in the distribution of native endowments, any more than one deserves one's initial starting place in society. The assertion that a man deserves the superior character that enables him to make the effort to cultivate his abilities is equally problematic; for his character depends in large part upon fortunate family and social circumstances for which he can claim no credit. The notion of desert seems not to apply to these cases. Thus the more advantaged representative man cannot say that he deserves and therefore has a right to a scheme of cooperation in which he is permitted to acquire benefits in ways that do not contribute to the welfare of others. There is no basis for his making this claim.[6]

Similarly, Rawlsian justice requires that while inequalities of position can exist, the higher positions must be open to all.

> I shall now state in a provisional form the two principles of justice that I believe would be chosen in the original position. In this section I wish to make only the most general comments, and therefore the first formulation of these principles is tentative. As we go on I shall run through several formulations and approximate step by step the final statement to be given much later. I believe that doing this allows the exposition to proceed in a natural way.
>
> The first statement of the two principles reads as follows.
>
>> First: each person is to have an equal right to the most extensive basic liberty compatible with a similar liberty for others.
>>
>> Second: social and economic inequalities are to be arranged so that they are both (a) reasonably expected to be to everyone's advantage, and (b) attached to positions and offices open to all...
>
> The second principle applies, in the first approximation to the distribution of income and wealth and to the design of organizations that make use of differences

---

6   Rawls, A Theory of Justice, pp. 103-104.

in authority and responsibility, or chains of command. While the distribution of wealth and income need not be equal, it must be to everyone's advantage, and at the same time, positions of authority and offices of command must be accessible to all. One applies the second principle by holding positions open, and then, subject to this constraint, arranges social and economic inequalities so that everyone benefits.[7]

However, Rawls is careful to insist that these two principles are in serial order, with the first taking precedent to the second in case of any conflict. A just society will not violate individuals' political liberties even if it will enhance economic equality.

These principles are to be arranged in a serial order with the first principle prior to the second. This ordering means that a departure from the institutions of equal liberty required by the first principle cannot be justified by, or compensated for, by greater social and economic advantages. The distribution of wealth and income, and the hierarchies of authority, must be consistent with both the liberties of equal citizenship and equality of opportunity....The basic liberties of citizens are, roughly speaking, political liberty (the right to vote and to be eligible for public office) together with freedom of speech and assembly; liberty of conscience and freedom of thought; freedom of the person along with the right to hold (personal) property; and freedom from arbitrary arrest and seizure as defined by the concept of the rule of law. These liberties are all required to be equal by the first principle, since citizens of a just society are to have the same basic rights.[8]

Rawls finds a liberal Constitutional democracy with a Welfare State system of equal opportunity to be the most just.

...a common understanding of justice as fairness makes a constitutional democracy. For I have tried to show, after presenting further arguments for the first principle, that the basic liberties of a democratic regime are most firmly secured by this conception of justice.[9]

Rawls identifies benefits of a capitalist economy, but admits that a democratic socialist regime could also satisfy the principles of justice.

A further and more significant advantage of a market system is that, given the requisite background institutions, it is consistent with equal liberties and fair equality

---

7   Rawls, *A Theory of Justice*, pp. 60–61.
8   Rawls, *A Theory of Justice*, p. 61.
9   Rawls, *A Theory of Justice*, p. 243.

of opportunity. Citizens have a free choice of careers and occupations. There is no reason at all for the forced and central direction of labor. Indeed, in the absence of some differences in earnings as these arise in a competitive scheme, it is hard to see how, under ordinary circumstances anyway, certain aspects of a command society inconsistent with liberty can be avoided. Moreover, a system of markets decentralizes the exercise of economic power. Whatever the internal nature of firms, whether they are privately or state owned, or whether they are run by entrepreneurs or by managers elected by workers, they take the prices of outputs and inputs as given and draw up their plans accordingly. When markets are truly competitive, firms do not engage in price wars or other contests for market power. In conformity with political decisions reached democratically, the government regulates the economic climate by adjusting certain elements under its control, such as the overall amount of investment, the rate of interest, and the quantity of money, and so on. There is no necessity for comprehensive direct planning. Individual households and firms are free to make their decisions independently, subject to the general conditions of the economy.[10]

So far I have assumed that the aim of the branches of government is to establish a democratic regime in which land and capital are widely though not presumably equally held. Society is not so divided that one fairly small sector controls the preponderance of productive resources. When this is achieved and distributive shares satisfy the principles of justice, many socialist criticisms of the market economy are met. But it is clear that, in theory anyway, a liberal socialist regime can also answer to the two principles of justice. We have only to suppose that the means of production are publicly owned and that firms are managed by workers' councils say, or by agents appointed by them. Collective decisions made democratically under the constitution determine the general features of the economy, such as the rate of saving and the proportion of society's production devoted to essential public goods.[11]

Social Ethics

For Rawls, the good society is one characterized by justice as defined in *A Theory of Justice*, and a good person is one who supports its principles of liberty and inequality for the benefit of the least advantaged. This, then, forms an ideal to which existing societies may strive.

> Viewing the theory of justice as a whole, the ideal part presents a conception of a just society that we are to achieve if we can. Existing institutions are to be judged

---

10 Rawls, *A Theory of Justice*, pp. 272–273.
11 Rawls, *A Theory of Justice*, p. 280.

in the light of this conception and held to be unjust to the extent that they depart from it without sufficient reason. The lexical ranking of the principles specifies which elements of the ideal are relatively more urgent, and the priority rules this ordering suggests are to be applied to nonideal cases as well. Thus as far as circumstances permit, we have a natural duty to remove any injustices, beginning with the most grievous as identified by the extent of the deviation from perfect justice. Of course, this idea is extremely rough. The measure of departures from the ideal is left importantly to intuition. Still our judgment is guided by the priority indicated by the lexical ordering. If we have a reasonably clear picture of what is just, our considered convictions of justice may fall more closely into line even though we cannot formulate precisely how this greater con vergence comes about. Thus while the principles of justice belong to the theory of an ideal state of affairs, they are generally relevant.[12]

For Rawls, then, some social and economic inequality is inevitable, given individual differences. The most we can ask for is not the total elimination of inequality, but that the inequalities that do exist are to the benefit of the poorest. If society provides equal opportunity for individuals of all classes to develop their skills and talents through public education, and if the higher positions are open to all according to merit, the individual who fails to succeed will have no one to blame but himself. This, for Rawls, will diminish the instances of envy of the rich by the poor and contribute to a stable regime.

> After all, if the disposing conditions for envy are removed, so probably are those for jealousy, grudgingness, and spite, the converses of envy. When the less fortunate segments of society lack the one, the more fortunate will lack the other. Taken together these features of a well-ordered regime diminish the number of occasions when the less favored are likely to experience their situation as impoverished and humiliating. Even if they have some liability to envy, it may never be strongly evoked.[13]

> There are three conditions, I assume, that encourage hostile outbreaks of envy. The first of these is the psychological condition we have just noted: persons lack a sure confidence in their own value and in their ability to do anything worthwhile. Second (and one of two social conditions), many occasions arise when this psychological condition is experienced as painful and humiliating. The discrepancy between oneself and others is made visible by the social structure and style of life of one's society. The less fortunate are therefore often forcibly reminded of their situation, sometimes leading them to an even lower estimation of themselves and their

---

12 Rawls, *A Theory of Justice*, p. 246.
13 Rawls, *A Theory of Justice*, p. 537.

mode of living. And third, they see their social position as allowing no constructive alternative to opposing the favored circumstances of the more advantaged. To alleviate their feelings of anguish and inferiority, they believe they have no choice but to impose a loss on those better placed even at some cost to themselves, unless of course they are to relapse into resignation and apathy.

Now many aspects of a well-ordered society work to mitigate if not to prevent these conditions. In regard to the first condition, it is clear that, although it is a psychological state, social institutions are a basic instigating cause. But I have maintained that the contract conception of justice supports the self-esteem of citizens generally more firmly than other political principles. In the public forum each person is treated with the respect due to a sovereign equal; and everyone has the same basic rights that would be acknowledged in an initial situation regarded as fair. The members of the community have a common sense of justice and they are bound by ties of civic friendship. I have already discussed these points in connection with stability. We can add that the greater advantages of some are in return for compensating benefits for the less favored; and no one supposes that those who have a larger share are more deserving from a moral point of view.[14]

I conclude, then, that the principles of justice are not likely to arouse excusable general envy (nor particular envy either) to a troublesome extent. By this test, the conception of justice again seems relatively stable.[15]

Thus, Rawls' "justice as fairness" provides equal liberty to all, rewards to the gifted and industrious, and compensations to the poor.

---

14 Rawls, A *Theory of Justice*, pp. 535–536.
15 Rawls, A *Theory of Justice*, p. 537.

Epilogue

A (Possible) Future Political Theory: The Web of Globalism

There seems (in 2021) to be no comprehensive, coherent, and widely accepted new Political Theory of our time, with a completely developed, consistent definition of Human Nature; Political Society; and Social Ethics, as was present in Rawls' Theory of Liberalism, Marx's Communism, or Aristotle's Classical Democracy.

The closest might be an edited book by two British scholars at Durham University: *Global Political Theory*. Ironically, they link this Theory to Rawls' Theory of Justice by advocating a system of "lives more interconnected than ever...[an] uninterrupted chain of physical, economic, political, and ultimately moral relationships with strangers on all parts of the globe" (web: *Globalization and Global Political Theory*).

Also, there are definite social and political trends over the past 30 years that point to an emerging systematic theory reminiscent of the Classics in this book. These trends include the worldwide web or internet, distant online commerce, entertainment, education, medicine, work, and human relationships that might be termed "The Web of Globalism." The key feature of this new system and the philosophy describing and justifying it is the elimination of national, cultural, historical, religious, and economic differences in a One World Order.

It transforms life, work, learning, relationships, by eliminating onsite small-scale, local organizations (marriage, family, community, business, school) with a world in which each individual relates to the other 8 billion humans on earth through partial, temporary, online interactions across the globe. Communication, transportation, commerce, etc. no longer occur between humans in a spatially close (e. g. sitting in the same room) temporally semi-permanent (friendships, groups, romance, marriage, family, school, occupational) situation, but in multiple distant, partial, and temporary settings.

A new flexible but impersonal human contact (remote work, distance learning, online relationships, internet commerce and entertainment) may characterize this "New World Order." The COVID-19 Pandemic of 2020-21 accelerated the process as the shutdown of traditional society advanced the distance web activities. In terms of the three categories examining the Classics of Political Theory (1. Human Nature, 2. Political Society, and 3. Social Ethics) this Global Web Theory may contain the following.

1. Human Nature. Rather than emphasizing Reason (Aristotle), Production (Marx), Freedom and Property (Locke), the new human seems to be defined as a universal world being primarily as a consumer. "Shopping" or browsing on the Web for information, entertainment, products and services, and knowledge with other global human beings. The current emphasis on "Diversity and Inclusion" along with "Equity" encourages this universal worldwide human, without definition by nationality, culture, religion, race, gender, accomplishments, or background. Even distinct qualifications or traits may be subordinated to the collective of uniform World Humanity. Such distant, impersonal, isolated humanity may be seen as the height of "alienation" from self and others or the "liberation" of the human species. All individuals provided with basic needs (food, housing, medicine, etc.) by advanced automated technology may seem the fulfillment of Marx's Communist Utopia or his final stage of capitalism in which everyone becomes a "commodity," having to sell oneself on the market as a product.

A satirical, artistic portrayal of this universalism may be the film, "Sleeper," in which a man is awakened after a 200-year coma to find automation and robotics providing basic services to all equally, including a condominium for each person ("as it has been scientifically proven that people get on each other's nerves."). A comfortable but controlled and mediocre universal individual. In this film a nascent revolutionary guerilla movement forms to overthrow the all-controlling state.

2. Political Society. The governing order of this World Web is obviously global, international, and electronic. Perhaps institutions like the U.N., the World Health Organization, World Court of Justice, etc. will order and rule everything. Regulated societies into central global control, central social indexing of behavior, speech, and thought and regulation of all economic, climate, health, behavior, and progress may suggest this ideal new system of politics. For some, this is global justice; for others, totalitarian tyranny. The embracing of this remote, impersonal life may remind some of C.S. Lewis, the philosopher and Oxford don, who wrote that when food rationing ended after World War II, many people had come to prefer tinned meat to fresh food. We may already prefer ZOOM meetings and remote relationships to personal contact.

3. Social Ethics. The "good" person and citizen in such a system would obviously accept and contribute to it. The moral norms would be working within this Global Order, not distracting from it or subverting it with national, religious, cultural, traditional standards contrary to this prevailing system. This may seem exclusionary of some valuable human traits (individual thought and action contrary to the global standard) but is hard for someone living in a remote American rural area who can order Belgian Chocolate Truffles online and have them delivered to his door the next day to be wholly critical.

Still, this emerging Global Web society may be critiqued by some former Greats in Political Theory, such as Aristotle, St. Augustine, Aquinas, Locke, Burke, Karl Marx, Gentile, and Hannah Arendt.

Classical Critiques of Web Globalism

Aristotle proclaimed that humans are by nature rational, social, and ethical beings. To develop these qualities (Telos) and thereby usefulness, fulfilment, and happiness, they must have a certain environment, education, and activity. Human capacities are refined in private life (household, family, friendship) and public life (politics, participation in governance) within small democratic communities. These require personal, long-term relationships to develop one's gifts and contribute to the good of society as well as one's own good. This Aristotelean philosophy might be troubled by the partial, fragmented, and temporary quality of web globalism. Millions of contacts over great distances for brief encounters may not develop the human "soul" (psyche) as would more stable, close, permanent commitments in more immediate relationships in marriage, family, education, work, and citizenship.

St. Augustine's Christian Political Theology regarded ALL worldly governments, regardless of time, place, or structure as tainted with pride, sin, greed, corruption, and oppression. A system of global communication, commerce, and control would not be immune from these worldly qualities and, no matter how universal and inclusive, may be even more oppressive than previous regimes. Only the transcendent City of God is perfect justice, peace, and equity, and only those earthly regimes that strive for it are tolerably just.

St. Thomas Aquinas's Three Laws (Divine, Natural, and Human) are a relatively permanent standard of private and public morality, taught by Tradition, Experience, Scripture, and Reason. The absence of these qualities will make web globalism chaotic and unjust, causing illness (mental and physical) and injustice.

For Locke, and the liberal democracies promised in his Natural Rights Philosophy, individual Liberty, Property, and Freedom in a Social Contract with a "limited Government" to protect those rights is necessary to personal, intellectual, economic, religious, and political functioning and happiness. Web globalism, with its intertwined and tightly controlled relationships may seem tyrannical to him.

Edmund Burke's Organic Conservatism sees traditional culture and society passing on the most valuable knowledge and accomplishments of human history as permanent and best. Any system that destroyed such historical excellence would be unjust, or rather impossible. The institutions and practices that reflected the best in human nature would emerge in some form, albeit possibly exaggerated or perverted. If natural human needs were not satisfied in a healthy way, they would be "satisfied" in an unhealthy, incomplete manner. Return to the best of the past is preferable to a Burkean conservative, but the web globalism may preserve that, if only partially and selectively.

Karl Marx, the Father of Communism, as noted, may celebrate the technological advances of the new system and see the support of basic needs through the global economy as liberating for individuals who no longer have to work for survival and can develop their gifts and abilities to the common good. The potential control and censorship of the system, as well as the seeming requirement of everyone to "sell" themselves continually on the internet "market" may give pause to Marx for its Final Stage of Capitalism image or turning everyone into a "Commodity" or product to receive social rewards.

One question that this might pose is "when" one can fully participate in this system. Do children have full access to its demands and benefits. Mentally challenged or criminals? Or does the system effectively regulate them? Gentile's fascism may admire the "Universal" quality of humanity in Globalism, but object to its not being nationalistic.

Finally, Hannah Arendt, whom I consider the greatest political philosopher of the 20th century, captures in her book, *The Human Condition*, the most comprehensive portrayal of human nature and society since Aristotle. Her definitions of the "Private" realms (home, family, friendship) and "Public" realm (political discourse in small democratic communities) needed for human fulfillment, being inverted by "society," which makes previously private aspects of human life "public" and reduces "public" political life to "private" concerns (interest groups, lobbyists, etc.) corrupts both and poisons both individual life and democracy. The internet's surveillance and broadcasting world-wide formerly private matters and the manipulation of politics by private concerns may confirm Arendt's concerns.

Alas, only time will tell exactly what the future world order will be—its theoretical confirmation and its place in the History of Political Theory.

www.ingramcontent.com/pod-product-compliance
Lightning Source LLC
Chambersburg PA
CBHW071409300426
44114CB00016B/2242